D1599748

Intermediate Steps
to Understanding

L. A. Hill

Oxford University Press
外 國 語 研 修 社

Oxford University Press

Oxford London Glasgow
New York Toronto Melbourne Auckland
Kuala Lumpur Singapore Hong Kong Tokyo
Delhi Bombay Calcutta Madras Karachi
Nairobi Dar Es Salaam Cape Town
and associates in
Beirut Berlin Ibadan Mexico City Nicosia

© *Oxford University Press (Tokyo) 1980*

First published 1980
Seventh impression 1983

First Korean impression 1985

*All rights reserved. No part of this publication may be reproduced,
stored in a retrieval system, or transmitted, in any form or by any means,
electronic, mechanical, photocopying, recording or otherwise,
without the prior permission of Oxford University Press.*

*This reprint has been authorised by Oxford University Press for
sale in Korea only and not for export therefrom.*

ISBN 0 19 581854 7

Illustrated by Dennis Mallet

OXFORD is a trademark of Oxford University Press.

이 책은 당사가 한국내 독점출판권을 소유하고 있으므로 당사의 서면 허가
없이 그 일부 또는 전부의 복사 또는 전재를 금합니다.

Printed in Korea

영어의 표현력 및 이해력 양성에 역점을 둔 L.A.HILL 박사의
명저 Stories for Reproduction 총서 한국판을 내놓으면서

우리의 국력이 크게 신장되어 국제 교류의 폭이 확대되어 감에 따라 각계 각층에서 영어에 능통한 인재의 요구가 날로 늘어가고 있읍니다. 그러나 이러한 실력을 갖춘 인재는 구하기가 쉽지 않을 뿐 아니라, 최고 학부를 나온 분들 마저 영어를 필요로 하는 업무에 부닥치면 **표현력**(말과 글로 표현하기)이나 **이해력**(읽거나 듣고 이해하기) 부족 때문에 많은 곤란을 겪고 있읍니다.

따지고 보면 이러한 현상이 생기게 된 것은 당연한 결과라고 할 수 있겠읍니다. 왜냐하면 지금까지의 영어 교육이 난해한 영문의 국역이나 까다로운 문법체계의 학습에 치중한 나머지 **작문력, 회화력, 독해력** 특히 **속독력** 및 **청해력** 등을 양성하는 학습을 소홀히 해 왔기 때문입니다.

그렇다면 영어의 **표현력**과 **이해력**을 기르기 위해서는 무엇부터 시작하여 어떻게 해야 하는지 그 구체적인 방법을 살펴 보기로 합시다.

1. 상용 2000 단어의 철저한 학습과 활용

영어로 일상적인 의사표시를 하는 데있어서는 빈도수가 높은 것만을 뽑아 만든 2,000 **상용 단어**만의 사용으로 부족함이 없읍니다. 예를 들면 6만의 표제어와 6만9천의 예문을 싣고 있는 **Longman Dictionary of Contemporary English**는 표제어의 정의와 그 예문을 제시하는 데 2,000의 「정의 어휘(Defining Vocabulary)」와 단순한 문법구조만을 쓰고 있으며, **Longman Dictionary of Business English**도 Michael West의 **상용 영어 단어 일람표**(A General Service List of English Words)를 토대로 한 2,000여 단어와 단순한 문법구조만으로 Business 각 분야의 전문용어를 완벽하게 해설하고 있읍니다.

이런 사실만을 보아도 영어 실력 양성에 있어서 **2,000상용 단어**의 **철저한 학습**과 그 **활용연습**이 얼마나 중요한 것이라는 것을 쉽게 이해할 수 있을 것입니다.

그럼에도 불구하고 이 **2,000상용 단어**의 철저한 기초학습이 채 끝나기도 전에, 일상적 의사표시에는 별로 쓰이지 않아 기억하기도 힘든 많은 어려운 영어 단어들(고교 수준에서는 약 5,000, 대학과 대학원 수준에서는 10,000~30,000단어)을 단편적, 기계적으로 암기하거나 난해한 영문의 국역이나 까다로운 문법체계의 학습에만 매달린다면 아무리 노력을 해 봤자 모래 위에 성을 쌓는 격이어서, 영어로 자신의 생각을 자유롭게 **표현**할 수 있는 정도까지 그 실력이 향상되기를 기대할 수 없는 것입니다.

2. 문맥적 접근법(Contextualized Approach)

어학의 습득은「의미내용」의「기억, 재현」과정을 통해 이루어지는 것이며, 이「의미내용」을 전달하는 효율은 1. 숫자(Figure) 2. 문자(Letter) 3. 단어(Word) 4. 문(Sentence) 5. 문장의 절(Paragraph)순으로, 그것이 함축하는「의미내용」의 차원이 높은 것일수록 그 전달량이 커지고 전달 효율이 높아집니다. 따라서 영어 학습에 있어서도 단어나 문법을 따로 학습하는 것보다는 문장내에서 문맥(Context)에 따라 이를 학습하는 것이 그 기억과 재현의 효율을 높일 수 있는 것입니다.

3. 표현력 향상을 위한 재현(Reproduction)연습

영어의 표현력을 기르는 데는 모범적인 영어 문장을 되풀이해서 읽고 이것을 재현(Reproduction)하는 연습을 해 보는 것이 가장 효과적이라는 것은 이미 널리 알려진 사실입니다. 그래서 중·고교의 교과서를 한 권이라도 암기해 보라고 권유하는 분들이 많으나, 이 교과서 자체가 암기와 재현 연습용으로 쓰기에는, 본문의 길이가 너무 길거나 난해할 뿐 아니라 재현 연습을 유도하는 적절한 Questions, Exercises 및 Answer Key 등의 뒷받침이 되어 있지 않기 때문에 표현력 향상을 위한 교재로는 적합하지 못합니다.

영어 교육계의 오랜 경험에서 밝혀진 바에 의하면 표현력 양성을 목적으로 하는 영어 문장 재현 연습용의 교재는 다음과 같은 요건을 갖춘 것이 가장 효과가 높다는 것입니다.

첫째 교재 본문의 내용이 학습자의 지속적인 흥미와 관심을 끌 수 있을 만큼 재미 있으면서도 교육적 가치가 풍부한 것이어야 하며,

둘째 교재에 사용되는 단어, 숙어, 문법구조등이 각 학습단계(입문, 초급, 중급, 상급수준 등)에 꼭 알맞게 제한 사용되어야 하며,

셋째 재현 연습에 쓰일 본문의 길이도 기억과 재현에 알맞는 단어수(학습 단계에 따라 150 단어 내지 350 단어의 길이)를 초과하지 않아야 하고,

넷째 학습시키고자 하는 단어, 숙어, 문법구조등이 교재의 본문에 흡수·통합되어 이 것들이 각기 따로 따로 유리되어 있을 때 보다 높은 차원의「의미내용」을 갖도록 하여야 한다는 것입니다.

따라서 영어의 표현력과 이해력의 종합적인 향상을 위해서는 무엇보다 먼저 위에 열거한 네가지 요건을 갖춘 교재가 절대 필요한 것입니다. 그런데 이러한 교재의 입수가 지극히 어렵던 차에, 다행히 옥스포드대학출판부에서, 이 방면의 세계적 권위자인 L.A.HILL 박사로 하여금 위에 적은 네가지 요건을 모두 갖춘 영어 학습교재 총서를 저술케하여, 이를 최근에 모두 펴 내놓아 외국어로서영어를 배우는 전세계 영어학도들의 절

찬을 받고 있는 것을 보고, 실용 영어의 통신교육과 그에 부수되는 영어 교재의 출판을 전문으로 하고 있는 저희 外國語研修社에서는, 이 교재의 한국내 출판이 저희들의 사업목적에 부합될 뿐 아니라 이러한 교재를 찾고 있는 수 많은 독자와 영어 교사들에게 크게 도움이 되리라고 생각하고 작년부터 옥스포드대학출판부와 판권 교섭을 해 오던 끝에 금년들어 계약이 성립되어 **L. A. HILL** 박사 저술의 영어 학습 교재중 **표현력 및 이해력** 향상에 역점을 둔 교재 전 **4** 집을 아래와 같이 내놓게 되었읍니다.

제 **1** 집 **Stories for Reproduction 1** : 입문편, 초급편, 중급편 및 상급편의 Text 각 1 권과 그 Study Guide(학습안내서)각 1 권 및 이에 딸린 음성교재용 녹음테이프.

제 **2** 집 **Stories for Reproduction 2** : 입문편, 초급편, 중급편 및 상급편의 Text 각 1 권과 그 Answer Key 각 1 권 및 이에 딸린 음성교재용 녹음테이프.

제 **3** 집 **Steps to Understanding** : 입문편, 초급편, 중급편 및 상급편의 Text 각 1 권과 그 Answer Key 각 1 권 및 이에 딸린 음성교재용 녹음테이프.

제 **4** 집 **Stories for Reproduction (American Series)** : 초급편, 중급편 및 상급편의 Text 각 1 권과 그 Answer Key 및 이에 딸린 음성교재용 녹음테이프.

전 세계적인 Best Seller 가 되어 있는 이 교재는 표현력과 독해력 향상에 필수적인 단어·숙어와 문법구조를 4 단계로 나누어 제한 사용하고 있어 독자들에게 학습상의 부담을 주지 않을 뿐 아니라 그 본문이 유우머(해학)와 윗트(기지)로 가득찬 흥미진진한 짧은 이야기로 되어 있기 때문에 그것을 끝까지 단숨에 읽을 수 있도록 되어 있으며, 이 이야기를 속독, 청취, 정독, 재청(再聽)한 다음 다양한 **Questions**와 **Exercises** 를 사용한 문답식 방법으로 그 내용을 이해하는 훈련을 쌓는 동시에 이를 다시 말과 글로 표현해 보는(**Oral & Written Reproduction**)연습을 되풀이 함으로써, 난해한 영문국역, 단편적인 단어·숙어의 암기나 문법체계의 학습등에서 오는 정신적 긴장과 피로를 수반하지 않고, 독자들이 이야기의 내용을 즐기다 보면 자기도 모르는 사이에 이해력과 표현력이 몸에 붙도록 꾸며져 있읍니다.

또한 이 교재는 Text와는 따로 **Study Guide**(학습안내서), **Answer Key** (해답집) 및 녹음테이프가 딸려 있어 개인의 자습(Self-Study)용으로는 물론 교실 수업용으로도 쓸 수 있도록 만들어져 있읍니다.

이 교재가 많은 독자들의 영어 표현력 및 이해력 향상에 획기적인 도움이 되기를 바랍니다.

1985년 1월 5일

外國語研修社
代表理事
會　長　李　瀅　載

머 리 말

이 책은 흥미진진하면서 평이한 이야기를 읽거나 듣고 그 내용을 기억하여 자신의 말과 글로 다시 표현해 봄으로써 영어의 이해력(讀解 · 聽解)과 표현력(作文 · 會話)을 기를 것을 목적으로 쓰여졌던 **Stories for Reproduction Series**(이야기의 재현을 통해 배우는 영어 총서)의 속편으로서 그 제 3 집에 해당되는 **Steps to Understanding**(영어 이해의 4 단계)의 제 3 단계(중급편)이며 1,500 표제어 수준으로 쓰여져 있습니다.

이야기의 길이는 대략 150 단어 정도이고 수록된 이야기들 중에는 1,500 표제어 수준을 넘는 단어 한 두개가 들어 있는 것들도 약간 있습니다. 이 단어들은 각기 해당된 이야기가 수록된 페이지의 하단에 나열되어 있으니 공부를 시작하기 전에 사전에서 찾아 보실 수 있겠읍니다. 각 단계마다 단어 뿐만 아니라 숙어와 문법도 또한 각 단계에 알맞도록 주의 깊게 제한 사용되어 있읍니다.

목적

이 네 권의 책들은 학생들이 영어를 좀더 용이하게 읽고 좀더 **정확하게 이해하도록** 돕는 것을 주목적으로 하여 쓰여진 것이나 다음과 같은 목적으로도 이용할 수 있겠읍니다.

(ⅰ) 듣고 이해하기(聽解) 연습

(선생님이 읽어 주는 이야기를 듣거나 카셋트를 듣고) 구어영어(口語英語 – **Spoken English**)를 이해하는 연습;

(ⅱ) 영작문(英作文) 연습

(이야기 내용에 대한 질의문을 영어로 해답하고; 이야기를 최대한으로 기억하여 써 보며; 연습문제를 풀어 봄으로써) 영어로 글을 쓰는 연습;

(ⅲ) 어휘, 숙어, 문법의 구사력(語彙, 熟語, 文法의 驅使力) 향상

(특정한 연습문제를 풀어 봄으로써) 학생들이 어휘(**Vocabulary**) 관용어법(**Idioms**) 및 문법(**Grammar**)을 자유로히 활용할 수 있는 능력을 향상시킬 목적 등.

공부하는 방법

이 책을 독해(讀解) 연습용으로만 사용하고자 할 경우에는 이야기를 읽고 그 내용에 대한 질의문(Questions)을 자국어로 대답해 보면 되겠읍니다.

또한 질의문의 전부 또는 일부를 먼저 읽고 난 후, 질의문에 답하기 전에 이야기를 읽

으면서 그 안에서 해답을 찾아 볼 수도 있겠읍니다. 읽는 속도를 올리기 위하여 시간을 재가면서 이해가 가능한 최대한의 속도로 읽는(속독-速讀) 연습을 해 볼 수도 있겠읍니다.

이 책을 구어영어(**Spoken English**)를 이해하기 위한 연습(**Speaking with Good Pronunciation & Listening Comprehension**)용으로 쓸 경우에는 카셋트를 다음과 같은 방법으로 쓸 수 있겠읍니다.

(i) (책을 펴 놓거나 덮어 놓고) 카셋트를 1 회 또는 그 이상 듣고 난 후, 처음에는 카셋트에 마춰 가며 이야기를 소리 내어 읽고, 다음에는 카셋트를 틀지 않고 혼자서 소리내어 읽어 봅니다. 다 읽고 난 후에는 카셋트를 다시 들으면서 강세(**Stress**) 리듬(**rhythm**) 및 억양(**Intonation**)등을 포함하여 발음이 정확히 되었는지 자세히 살펴 봅니다.

(ii) 책을 덮고 카셋트를 1 회 또는 그 이상 들은 다음 그 내용을 기억할 수 있는 최대한까지 공책에 써 보고/써보거나 이야기를 보지 않고 질의문에 답하고 연습문제를 풀어봅니다. 이야기를 기억하여 최대한으로 쓰고 난 후에는 책에 있는 이야기를 보거나 카셋트를 다시 들어 보고 이야기의 원본과 자신이 기억해 쓴 것을 비교해 봅니다.

(i)의 방법으로 강세, 리듬, 억양을 포함하여 정확한 발음으로 말하는 연습을 하게 됩니다.

(ii)의 방법으로는 청해(聽解-듣고 이해하기) 연습을 하게 됩니다.

L. A. Hill 박사가 1,500표제어 수준으로 쓴 교재에는 다음과 같은 것들이 있읍니다.

Word Power 3,000: Vocabulary Tests and Exercieses in American English

Intermediate Stories for Reproduction, Series 1

Intermediate Stories for Reproduction, Series 2

Intermediate Stories for Reproduction, American Series.

Intermediate Comprehension Topics

Oxford Graded Readers, 1,500-Headword level: Junior and Senior Stories

Introduction

In his earlier series' of practice books*, Dr. Hill has used three levels, his elementary (1 000-headword), intermediate (1 500-headword) and advanced (2 075-headword) levels. In this new series, however, there is also another level, the introductory (750-headword) level. This book is at the 1 500-headword level.

Each story is about 150 words long, and some of the stories contain one or two words outside the grading. These are listed on the pages on which they appear, and can be looked up in a dictionary before work is begun. All the levels are very carefully graded, and this covers not only vocabulary, but also idioms and grammar.

These four books are intended chiefly to help students read English more easily and with more comprehension, but they can also be used:

(i) for practice in understanding spoken English (with the student listening to the teacher or to the cassette);

(ii) for practice in writing English (by answering the questions in English; by writing as much of the story as the student can remember; and by doing the exercises); and

(iii) for improving the student's command of vocabulary, idioms and grammar (again by doing certain of the exercises).

If the student wishes to use the books *only* for practice in reading comprehension, he/she should read a story and then answer questions *in his/her mother-tongue*.

He/She can also try reading some (or all) of the questions *first*, and then reading the story to find the answers to the questions before answering them. To increase speed of reading, the student can time himself/herself with a watch or clock, and try to read as fast as possible, *provided that he/she can still understand*.

If the student wants to use this book for practice in understanding spoken English, he/she can use the cassette in the following ways:

*Stories for Reproduction, Series 1 and 2 and *Elementary* and *Intermediate Comprehension Pieces*, all published by Oxford University Press.

(i) He/She can listen to the cassette one or more times (with his/her book open or closed, as he/she wishes) and then read the story aloud himself/herself, at first in chorus with the voice on the cassette, and then alone. After his/her own reading alone, he/she can check his/her performance by listening to the cassette again.

(ii) He/She can listen to the cassette one or more times, with his/her book closed, and then write down as much of the story as he/she can remember, and/or answer the questions and do the exercises (all without looking at the story). If he/she writes as much of the story as he/she can remember, he/she can then look at the story in the book, or listen to it again on the cassette, to compare what he/she has written with the original.

Method (i) gives practice in speaking with a good pronunciation, including stress, rhythm and intonation.

Method (ii) gives practice in aural comprehension (listening and understanding).

Other books by Dr. L. A. Hill at his 1 500-headword level are:
Intermediate Comprehension Topics
Intermediate Stories for Reproduction (Series 1 and 2)
Oxford Graded Readers, 1 500-headword level: Junior and Senior Stories

Intermediate Steps
to Understanding

1

Mr and Mrs Taylor had one child. He was a boy, he was seven years old, and his name was Pat. Now Mrs Taylor was expecting another child.

Pat had seen babies in other people's houses and had not liked them very much, so he was not delighted about the news that there was soon going to be one in his house too.

One evening Mr and Mrs Taylor were making plans for the baby's arrival. 'This house won't be big enough for us all when the baby comes. I suppose we'll have to find a larger house and move to that,' said Mr Taylor finally.

Pat had been playing outside, but he came into the room just then and said, 'What are you talking about?'

'We were saying that we'll have to move to another house now, because the new baby's coming,' his mother answered.

'It's no use,' said Pat hopelessly. 'He'll follow us there.'

A **Which of these sentences are true (T) and which are false (F)? Write T or F in the boxes.**

1. Mr and Mrs Taylor had a son. ☐
2. Pat was five years old. ☐
3. Mrs Taylor was going to have another baby. ☐
4. Pat did not like babies. ☐
5. Pat was not happy about the new baby. ☐
6. Mr and Mrs Taylor lived in a large house. ☐

B **Answer these questions:**

1. Did Pat have any brothers or sisters at the beginning of this story?
2. Why was he not happy to hear that his mother was expecting a baby?
3. What did his father say one evening about the baby's arrival?
4. Where was Pat when his father said this?
5. What did he do?
6. What did he ask?
7. What did his mother answer?
8. What did Pat answer?

C **Write this story. Put one word in each empty place. You will find all the correct words in the story on page 4.**

Before Mr Taylor married, he lived in a very small flat, but when he married, it was no . . . trying to live there with a wife, so he had to . . . to a . . . flat. He was . . . to have a lot of trouble finding one, so he was . . . when he found one easily. Then he had to make . . . for moving his furniture. He also ordered more from a shop in a town, but he had to wait a month for its . . . , because it had to come from the north of England. I . . . he was lucky to have to wait only one month. Some people wait . . . month after month, and finally give up.

2

An important businessman went to see his doctor because he could not sleep at night. The doctor examined him carefully and then said to him, 'Your trouble is that you need to learn to relax. Have you got any hobbies?'

The businessman thought for a few moments and then said, 'No, doctor, I haven't. I don't have any time for hobbies.'

'Well,' the doctor answered, 'that is your main trouble, you see. You don't have time for anything except your work. You must find some hobbies, and you must learn to relax with them, or you'll be dead in less than five years. Why don't you learn to paint pictures?'

'All right, doctor,' the businessman said. 'I'll try that.'

The next day he telephoned the doctor and said, 'That was a very good idea of yours, doctor. Thank you very much. I've already painted fifteen pictures since I saw you.'

A   Which of these sentences are true (T) and which are false (F)? Write T or F in the boxes.

1. The businessman wanted to sleep less at night. □
2. The businessman had trouble in sleeping at night because he did not relax enough. □
3. The businessman did not have any hobbies, because he wanted to relax when he was not busy. □
4. The doctor said that he would be dead in five years

Outside the 1 500 headwords: relax

unless he learned some hobbies and relaxed while he was doing them. □

5. The doctor advised him not to do anything except his work, or he would be dead in less than five years. □

6. The businessman started a hobby, but he did not relax while he was doing it. □

B Answer these questions:

1. Why did the businessman go to his doctor?
2. What did the doctor tell him? (He told him that . . . .)
3. What did the businessman answer?
4. What did the doctor say was the businessman's main trouble?
5. What did he advise him to do?
6. What did he say would happen if he did not follow his advice?
7. What did the businessman answer?
8. What did he tell the doctor the next day on the telephone?

C *Hobbies.* **Make eight sentences out of this, and put each under the correct picture:**

| This | girl's man's woman's | hobby is | a. catching
b. climbing
c. collecting
d. doing
e. growing
f. keeping
g. painting
h. playing | i. fish.
ii. flowers.
iii. mountains.
iv. nothing.
v. pictures.
vi. rabbits.
vii. stamps.
viii. the trumpet. |

7

3

Mary's mother was nearly seventy, and Mary and her husband wanted to give the old lady a nice birthday present. She liked drinking tea, so Mary ordered an electric machine which made the tea and then woke you up in the morning. She wrapped it up in pretty paper and brought it to her mother on her birthday. Then her mother opened the package. Mary showed her how to use it.

'Before you go to bed, put the tea in the pot and the water in the kettle,' she explained to the old lady, 'and don't forget to switch the electricity on. Then, when you wake up in the morning, your tea will be ready.'

After a few days, Mary's mother rang up and said, 'Perhaps I'm being rather silly, but there's one thing I'm confused about: why do I have to go to bed to make the tea?'

A   Which of these sentences are true (T) and which are false (F)? Write T or F in the boxes.

   1. Mary's mother was old.

   2. She did not like tea very much.

Outside the 1 500 headwords: kettle

3. Mary sent her mother a nice present by post. ☐
4. The machine switched itself on in the morning. ☐
5. The kettle did not need electricity. ☐
6. Mary's mother thought she could only make the tea when
she was in bed. ☐

B   Answer these questions:

1. How old was Mary's mother?
2. What did Mary and her husband buy her mother?
3. Why did they choose this for her?
4. What could the machine do?
5. What happened when Mary brought her mother the present?
6. What did Mary tell her mother?
7. What did Mary's mother do a few days later?
8. What did she tell Mary on the telephone?

C   Put the correct sentences under the correct pictures:

1. Her mother opened it.
2. In the morning, she woke up, and the tea was ready.
3. Mary showed her how to use the machine.
4. Mary's mother switched the electricity on.
5. Mary went to a shop and ordered a tea-making machine.
6. Then she took it to her mother.
7. Then she went to bed.
8. When it came, she wrapped it up.

4

Mr Grey was the manager of a small office in London. He lived in the country, and came up to work by train. He liked walking from the station to his office unless it was raining, because it gave him some exercise.

One morning he was walking along the street when a stranger stopped him and said to him, 'You may not remember me, sir, but seven years ago I came to London without a penny in my pockets. I stopped you in this street and asked you to lend me some money, and you lent me five pounds, because you said that you were willing to take a chance so as to give a man a start on the road to success.'

Mr Grey thought for a few moments and then said, 'Yes, I remember you. Go on with your story.'

'Well,' answered the stranger, 'are you still willing to take a chance?'

A **Which of these sentences are true (T) and which are false (F)? Write T or F in the boxes.**

1. Mr Grey only walked to his office when the weather was good. □
2. He walked because he was poor. □
3. He had helped the stranger some years before. □
4. He had been willing to take a chance because he wanted to help the man. □
5. The stranger had been successful since then. □
6. Now he wanted to give Mr Grey his money back. □

B **Answer these questions:**

1. Where did Mr Grey work?
2. Where did he live?
3. How did he get from his home to his office?
4. Why didn't he go from the station to his office by bus every day?
5. What happened to him one day in the street?
6. What did the stranger say?
7. What did Mr Grey answer?
8. And what did the stranger ask then?

C **Answer these questions:**

1. What did the stranger say to Mr Grey? Begin your answer with the words, 'The stranger told Mr Grey that he . . . .'
2. What did Mr Grey answer? Begin your answer with the words, 'Mr Grey said that . . . .'
3. What did the stranger say then? Begin your answer with the words, 'The stranger asked him whether . . . .'

5

During the Second World War it was difficult to travel by plane, because the seats were needed for important government and army people.

Mr Brown worked for the government during the war. He was a civilian, and he was doing very secret work, so nobody was allowed to know how important he was except a very few people.

One day he had to fly to Edinburgh to give a lecture to a few top people there, but an important army officer came to the airport at the last minute, and Mr Brown's seat was given to him, so he was not able to fly to the city to give his lecture.

It was not until he reached the city that the important officer discovered that the man whose seat he had taken was the one whose lecture he had flown to the city to hear.

A   Which of these sentences are true (T) and which are false (F)? Write T or F in the boxes.

1. It was difficult for government and army people to find seats on planes during the Second World War. ☐
2. Mr Brown was an important person. ☐

Outside the 1 500 headwords: civilian (*n.*)

3. He wanted to go to Edinburgh by plane one day. ☐
4. His seat was given to somebody else because he was late. ☐
5. The important officer went to Edinburgh to give a lecture. ☐
6. The important officer arrived in time for Mr Brown's lecture, because he went by plane. ☐

B Answer these questions:

1. Why did ordinary people find it difficult to go by plane during the Second World War?
2. Whom did Mr Brown work for?
3. Was he in the army?
4. What work did he do?
5. Why were only very few people allowed to know how important he was?
6. Why did he have to fly somewhere one day?
7. Why didn't he manage to get there?
8. What did the important officer find out when he got to the city?

C Do this puzzle:

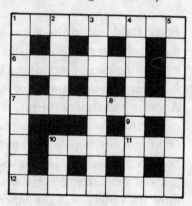

Across:
1. Not easy.
6. Put his foot.
7. Not the same.
8. Correct; right.
10. 'What hats do important officers . . . ?' 'They . . . hats like this:

11. If . . . the passengers had not come to the airport, Mr Brown could have got a seat.
12. There was plenty of room for the officer's legs in the plane, so he . . . them right out in front of him.

Down:
1. Finds.
2. Not stale.
3. The army officer was this, and Mr Brown was too.
4. The officer put his secret papers . . . his seat in the plane.
5. The officer . . . to the city, but Mr Brown did not.
9. . . . of the passengers had a ticket, but Mr Brown was not allowed to use his.
10. This story is about the Second World . . . .

6

Peter Judd joined the army when he was eighteen, and for several months he was taught how to be a good soldier. He did quite well in everything except shooting. One day he and his friends were practising their shooting, and all of them were doing quite well except Peter. After he had shot at the target nine times and had not hit it once, the officer who was trying to teach the young soldiers to shoot said, 'You're quite hopeless, Peter! Don't waste your last bullet too! Go behind that wall and shoot yourself with it!'

Peter felt ashamed. He went behind the wall, and a few seconds later the officer and the other young soldiers heard the sound of a shot.

'Heavens!' the officer said. 'Has that silly man really shot himself?'

He ran behind the wall anxiously, but Peter was all right. 'I'm sorry, sir,' he said, 'but I missed again.'

A   Which of these sentences are true (T) and which are false (F)? Write T or F in the boxes.

1. Peter was good at everything.
2. Peter was not good at shooting.

Outside the 1 500 headwords: shot (*n*.), target

3. A lot of the other soldiers were bad at shooting too. □
4. One of Peter's nine bullets hit the target. □
5. The officer was not pleased with him. □
6. The officer thought that Peter had shot himself. □

B Write these sentences. Choose the correct word in each:

1. Peter is looking at an enemy and trying to shoot
   { him.
   { himself.

2. Now Peter is trying to shoot
   { him.
   { himself.

3. Peter's girl-friend is sitting in front of her sister and making
   { her
   { herself } up.

4. Peter's girl-friend is sitting in front of her sister and making
   { her
   { herself } up.

5. The white donkey is in a field with a black donkey, and it has hurt
   { it.
   { itself.

6. The white donkey is in a field with a black one, and it has hurt
   { it.
   { itself.

7. The boys have brought their small sisters to a shop and bought
   { them
   { themselves } some sweets.

8. The boys have brought their small sisters to a shop and bought
   { them
   { themselves } some sweets.

15

7

Mr Richards worked in a small seaside town, and he and his wife had a comfortable house near the sea. During the winter they were quite happy there, but every summer a lot of their relatives used to want to come and stay with them, because it was a nice place for a holiday, and it was much cheaper than staying in a hotel.

Finally one June Mr Richards complained to an intelligent friend of his who lived in the same place. 'One of my wife's cousins intends to bring her husband and children and spend ten days with us next month again. How do you prevent all *your* relatives coming to live with you in the summer?'

'Oh,' the friend answered, 'that isn't difficult. I just borrow money from all the rich ones, and lend it to all the poor ones. After that, none of them come again.'

A Which of these sentences are true (T) and which are false (F)?
Write T or F in the boxes.

1. Mr and Mrs Richards did not have many relatives. ☐
2. Mr and Mrs Richards often went to stay with their
relatives in the summer. ☐
3. Mrs Richards's cousin decided to visit them. ☐
4. Mr Richards was not at all happy about this. ☐
5. A friend of his told him how to stop visitors. ☐
6. He borrowed money from his poor relatives, and lent
money to his rich ones. ☐

B Answer these questions:

1. Where did Mr and Mrs Richards live?
2. What was their house like?
3. Why were they happier in winter than in summer?
4. Why did their relatives want to visit them?
5. Who did Mr Richards ask for advice then?
6. What did he say to him?
7. And what did his friend answer?
8. Why did the friend's relatives not want to visit him again?

C Put one word in each empty place. You will find all the words in
the story on page 16.

George liked the sea, so he lived in a house at the . . . . His parents and a
lot of his other . . . lived near him. George's chairs were very hard, so
they were not very . . . to sit on. . . . one day his mother . . . about this,
saying, 'I wish you had some softer chairs, George.' But his father
laughed and answered, 'George is an . . . man: he has hard chairs
because he . . . to . . . people . . . too long when they come to visit him!
When he wants a soft chair, he can . . . it from our house.'

8

Mrs Scott bought a new house last year. The walls of the rooms had been painted a short time before, and Mrs Scott liked the colours, but the person who had sold her the house had taken the curtains with him, so Mrs Scott had to buy new ones, and of course she wanted to buy ones whose colours would go with the walls of her rooms. She discovered that her comb was exactly the same colour as these walls, so she always took it with her whenever she went to look for cloth for curtains.

In one shop she showed the shopkeeper the comb and then looked at various cloths for curtains for half an hour with him, until he got tired and said to her, 'Madam, wouldn't it be easier just to buy some cloth you like, and then find a new comb to go with that?'

A   Which of these sentences are true (T) and which are false (F)? Write T or F in the boxes.

1. When Mrs Scott bought her new house, she did not have the walls painted. ☐
2. She kept the curtains which the last owner had had. ☐
3. She liked curtains whose colour was rather like the walls. ☐
4. She liked curtains whose colour was very different from the walls. ☐
5. Her comb and the curtains were the same colour. ☐
6. Her comb and the walls were the same colour. ☐

7. One shopkeeper suggested that she should get a comb of a different colour instead of cloth like the comb. ☐

8. One shopkeeper suggested that she should buy some cloth which was like the comb and then find another comb which she liked. ☐

B Answer these questions:

1. Why did Mrs Scott not want to have the walls of her new house painted?
2. Why did she have to buy new curtains?
3. What kind of curtains did she want?
4. Why did she take her comb with her when she went looking for cloth?
5. What happened in one shop?
6. How did the shopkeeper feel after some time?
7. What did he say to Mrs Scott?
8. Why couldn't Mrs Scott follow his advice?

C *Moving into a new house.* **Make sentences to say where to put things in the house**.

'Please put that	a. armchair b. bookcase c. cooking-stove d. mirror e. razor f. refrigerator g. sewing-machine h. television i. toothpaste j. vase	in the	i. bathroom.' ii. bedroom.' iii. kitchen.' iv. living-room.'

9

Helen lived with her sister Mary. Both of them were about seventy-five years old, and neither of them had ever married. They had a small, old car, and when they wanted to go somewhere, which they did very rarely, Mary always drove, because her eyes were better.

One weekend they drove to a large town to look at some things which they had read about in the newspaper. Neither of them had been to that town before.

They were driving along in a lot of traffic when they turned right into a street which cars were not allowed to go into. There was a policeman there, and he blew his whistle, but Mary did not stop, so he got on to his motor-cycle and followed them.

After he had ordered them to stop, he said, 'Didn't you hear me blow my whistle?'

'Yes, we did,' admitted Mary politely, 'but Mummy told us never to stop when men whistle at us.'

A **Which of these sentences are true (T) and which are false (F)? Write T or F in the boxes.**

1. Helen and Mary were sisters. ☐
2. They were quite young. ☐
3. They were both married. ☐
4. Mary drove their car. ☐
5. A policeman tried to stop her one day. ☐
6. She did not stop, because she did not hear him blow his whistle. ☐

B **Answer these questions:**

1. Where did Mary and Helen drive one day?
2. What did they do in the town?
3. What did the policeman do?
4. And what did Mary do?
5. What did the policeman do then?
6. What did he say to Mary when he stopped her?
7. And what did Mary answer?
8. Had her mother really meant that she should not stop when a policeman blew his whistle?

C **Find words in the story on page 20 which mean about the same as:**

1. at any time
2. big
3. cars, buses, vans, etc.
4. confessed
5. got husbands
6. Mother
7. not rudely
8. Saturday or Sunday
9. seldom
10. told
11. went after

10

In England nobody under the age of eighteen is allowed to drink in a public bar.

Mr Thompson used to go to a bar near his house quite often, but he never took his son, Tom, because he was too young. Then when Tom had his eighteenth birthday, Mr Thompson took him to his usual bar for the first time. They drank for half an hour, and then Mr Thompson said to his son, 'Now, Tom, I want to teach you a useful lesson. You must always be careful not to drink too much. And how do you know when you've had enough? Well, I'll tell you. Do you see those two lights at the end of the bar? When they seem to have become four, you've had enough and should go home.'

'But, Dad,' said Tom, 'I can only see one light at the end of the bar.'

A   Which of these sentences are true (T) and which are false (F)? Write T or F in the boxes.

1. When Tom was under eighteen, his father took him to a public bar. ☐
2. It was the first time that he had taken him to his usual bar. ☐
3. There was one light at the end of the bar. ☐

4. Mr Thompson wanted to teach Tom not to drink too much. ☐
5. Mr Thompson thought he saw four lights. ☐
6. Tom only saw two. ☐

B   Answer these questions:

1. Who can drink in public bars in England?
2. Why did Mr Thompson not take Tom to his usual bar for a long time?
3. When *did* he take him?
4. What did they do there?
5. What did Mr Thompson say then?
6. And what did Tom answer?
7. Who had had enough to drink, Tom or his father?
8. How did Tom know this?

C   Put the correct sentences under the correct pictures:

1. But Tom could see only one.
2. He thought he could see two lights.
3. Mr Thompson used to go to a bar alone.
4. Then Mr Thompson pointed to the light at the end of the bar.
5. Then, when Tom was eighteen, he took him to the bar too.
6. They drank beer.

23

11

Mr and Mrs Davis had four children. One Saturday Mrs Davis said to her husband, 'The children haven't got any lessons today, and you're free too. There's a fun-fair in the park. Let's all go.'

Her husband was doubtful about this. 'I want to finish some work,' he said.

'Oh, forget about it and come to the fair!' his wife said.

So Mr and Mrs Davis took the children to the fun-fair. Mr Davis was forty-five years old, but he enjoyed the fun-fair more than the children. He hurried from one thing to another, and ate lots of sweets and nuts.

One of the children said to her mother, 'Daddy's behaving just like a small child, isn't he, Mummy?'

Mrs Davis was quite tired of following her husband around by now, and she answered, 'He's worse than a small child, Mary, because he's got his own money!'

A Which of these sentences are true (T) and which are false (F)? Write T or F in the boxes.

1. Mr Davis and his children did not work on Saturdays. □
2. Mr Davis was eager to go to the fun-fair, but his wife was not. □

Outside the 1 500 headwords: fun-fair

24

3. The children enjoyed the fun-fair, but Mr Davis did not. ☐
4. He behaved like a small child. ☐
5. Mrs Davis got tired. ☐
6. Mr Davis did not like the fun-fair because he was a rich man and wanted something better than that. ☐

B Answer these questions:

1. How many children did Mr and Mrs Davis have?
2. Where did Mrs Davis suggest that they should take them?
3. How did Mr Davis feel about this?
4. What did he say?
5. What did his wife answer?
6. What did he do at the fair?
7. What did one of the children say about him?
8. What did Mrs Davis answer?

C Choose the correct sentence for each picture:

1. Mr Davis is walking { along / among / between / through } a gate.

2. Mrs Davis is walking { along / among / between / through } a path.

3. Mrs Davis is standing { along / among / between / through } Mary and her brother.

4. Mr Davis is standing { along / among / between / through } his four children.

12

Mr Jones bought some things from a big shop last month, and when he got the bill a few days ago, he thought that there was a mistake in it, so he telephoned the shop and asked to speak to the Accounts Department. 'Who do you want to speak to in the Accounts Department?' the telephone operator asked.

'It doesn't matter to me,' Mr Jones answered. He did not know the names of any of the people who worked there. He heard nothing for a few seconds and then the operator said, 'Hullo, you wanted to speak to someone in the Accounts Department, didn't you?'

'Yes, that's right,' Mr Jones answered.

'Would you like to speak to Mr Hankinson?' the operator said.

'Yes, that'll be all right,' Mr Jones said patiently. 'It doesn't matter who I speak to.'

'I'm sorry,' the operator answered, 'but Mr Hankinson isn't in today.'

A Which of these sentences are true (T) and which are false (F)? Write T or F in the boxes.

1. Mr Jones got a bill from a big shop.
2. He believed that the bill was wrong.
3. He only knew Mr Hankinson in the Accounts Department.
4. The telephone operator tried to get Mr Hankinson for him.

Outside the 1 500 headwords: operator

5. Mr Hankinson was not in the Accounts Department that day. ☐

6. The telephone operator helped Mr Jones a lot. ☐

B Answer these questions:

1. Why did Mr Jones telephone the big shop?
2. What did the telephone operator ask him?
3. What did he answer?
4. What happened then?
5. What did Mr Jones say?
6. What did the operator ask him then?
7. What did Mr Jones answer?
8. And what did the operator say?

C Do this puzzle:

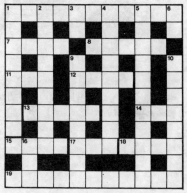

Across:

1. Mr Jones wanted to make an . . . to see somebody in the Accounts Department.
7. Big town.
8. In our country, most roofs are not flat: they . . . down on both sides.
11. We often . . . the telephone to order things from shops.
12.
13. Big shops keep their things in large . . .-rooms before they put them on the shelves.
14. Actors . . . in plays.
15. When someone telephones Mr Jones, he always . . . , '70532'.
17. Mr Jones pays his account at the shop by . . . month.
18. Not well.
19. 'Accounts' is one of the . . . in the big shop.

Down:

1. Mr Jones wanted to speak to someone in this department.
2. Mr Jones waited . . . for an answer, because he was not in a hurry.
3. There was a mistake . . . Mr Jones's bill.
4. and 9. Mr Jones spoke to the . . . . . in the big shop. (two words)
5. Mr Jones wanted an . . . of the mistake in his bill.
6. Mr Jones wanted . . . speak to someone in the Accounts Department.
9. See 4.
10. 'How many . . . were there in Mr Jones's bill?' 'One.'
16.

13

Mr Hodge was a chicken farmer. He had hundreds of chickens, and sold the eggs and the meat and got quite a lot of money for them, but he lived in a very hot part of the country, and he found that his hens laid hardly any eggs in the summer. So he decided to put air-conditioning into his chicken-house so that the hens would lay well all through the year and he could get more eggs and in that way earn more money.

The owner of the company which sold the air-conditioning came to see him, and when he saw Mr Hodge's house, he thought that he might be able to persuade him to buy some air-conditioning for that too.

'Your wife would be much happier and more comfortable then,' he said to Mr Hodge. But Mr Hodge was not interested.

'My wife doesn't lay eggs,' he said.

Outside the 1 500 headwords: air-conditioning

A **Which of these sentences are true (T) and which are false (F)? Write T or F in the boxes.**

1. Mr Hodge's chickens laid a lot of eggs when the weather was hot. □
2. Mr Hodge wanted air-conditioning for his chickens. □
3. The owner of the air-conditioning company sent a man to see Mr Hodge. □
4. The owner of the company wanted to sell as much air-conditioning as possible. □
5. Mr Hodge agreed to have air-conditioning in his house too. □
6. Air-conditioning in his house would not bring him more money. □

B **Answer these questions:**

1. What work did Mr Hodge do?
2. How did he earn his money?
3. Why did he not get so much money in the summer?
4. Where did he decide to put air-conditioning?
5. Why did he decide this?
6. What did the owner of the air-conditioning company hope to do?
7. What reason did he give for having air-conditioning in the house?
8. What did Mr Hodge answer?

C **Write these sentences. Choose the correct word or words to put in. The words are:** *could be earned, could earn, did not lay, put, sold, suggested, was put, was suggested, were laid, were sold.*

1. Mr Hodge . . . eggs and meat in the market.
2. Mr Hodge's eggs and meat . . . in the market.
3. The chickens . . . many eggs in summer.
4. Not many eggs . . . in summer.
5. Mr Hodge . . . more money if he had air-conditioning.
6. More money . . . by people who had air-conditioning.
7. The owner of the company . . . air-conditioning for the house too.
8. Air-conditioning for the house too . . . by the owner of the company.
9. Mr Hodge only . . . air-conditioning in his chicken-house.
10. Air-conditioning . . . only in Mr Hodge's chicken-house.

14

George Banks was a clever journalist. He worked for a good news-paper, and he liked arguing very much. He argued with anybody, and about anything. Sometimes the people whom he argued with were as clever as he was, but often they were not.

He did not mind arguing with stupid people at all: he knew that he could never persuade them to agree, because they could never really understand what he was saying; and the stupider they were, the surer they were that they were right; but he often found that stupid people said very amusing things.

At the end of one argument which George had with one of these less clever people, the man said something which George has always remembered and which has always amused him. It was, 'Well, sir, you should never forget this: there are always three answers to every question: your answer, my answer, and the correct answer.'

A **Which of these sentences are true (T) and which are false (F)? Write T or F in the boxes.**

1. George only argued with people who were less clever than he was. □
2. Stupid people understood what he said, because he spoke very clearly. □
3. Stupid people believed that they were always right. □
4. George was sometimes amused by stupid people. □
5. The stupid man thought that both he and George were wrong. □
6. George soon forgot what this man had said. □

B **Answer these questions:**

1. What was George's job?
2. What did he work for?
3. What was his hobby?
4. Why did he not mind arguing with stupid people?
5. How did stupid people argue?
6. Why did he enjoy that?
7. What did one stupid person say to George?
8. What did George think of this answer?

C **Find words in the story which mean about the same as:**

1. correct
2. funny
3. intelligent
4. less doubtful
5. made (him) laugh
6. make (them) believe
7. ought to
8. person who writes for a newspaper
9. talking against other people

15

Pat came over from Ireland to England with his wife one year to find work. He got quite a good job with a building company, and as he did not drink or smoke, he saved up quite a lot of money.

His wife's parents were still in Ireland, and one day she got a telegram to say that her mother was ill, so Pat gave her some money and she went to Ireland to see her.

After a week, Pat wanted to write a letter to her, but he could not read or write very well, so he went to his priest and asked him to do it for him. Pat told the priest what he wanted to say, and the priest wrote it down. After a few minutes Pat stopped, and the priest said, 'Do you want to say any more?'

'Only, "Please excuse the bad writing and spelling",' Pat said.

Outside the 1 500 headwords: priest

A Which of these sentences are true (T) and which are false (F)? Write T or F in the boxes.

1. Pat brought his wife to England with him. ☐
2. He did not spend all his money. ☐
3. His mother-in-law came to England too, because she was ill. ☐
4. Pat went to see his mother-in-law because she was ill. ☐
5. Pat wrote a letter to his wife after a week. ☐
6. He asked his wife to excuse the priest's bad writing and spelling. ☐

B Answer these questions:

1. Why did Pat come to England?
2. How did he manage to save money?
3. Why did his wife have to go to Ireland?
4. What did Pat want to do a week later?
5. Why didn't he write the letter?
6. Who wrote it for him?
7. What did the priest say after Pat had finished?
8. And what did Pat answer?

C Draw lines from the words on the left to the correct words on the right.

1. A building company   a. became ill.
2. Pat   b. could not read or write.
3. Pat's mother-in-law   c. gave Pat a job.
4. Pat's wife   d. went home to see her mother.
5. The priest   e. wrote Pat's letter.

Mark went to a barber's shop and had his hair cut, but when he came out, he was not happy with the result, and when his friend George saw him, he laughed and said, 'What's happened to your hair, Mark?'

Mark said, 'I tried a new barber's shop today, because I wasn't at all satisfied with my old one, but this one seems even worse.'

George agreed. 'Yes, I think you're right, Mark. Now I'll tell you what to do next time you go into a barber's shop: look at all the barbers' hair, and then go to the one whose own hair has been cut the worst.'

'The one whose hair's been cut the worst?' Mark repeated. 'But that would be foolish!'

'Oh, no, it wouldn't,' answered George. 'Who do you think cut that man's hair? He couldn't cut it himself, could he? Another of the barbers cut it—and he must have been a worse barber than the one whose hair he cut.'

A Which of these sentences are true (T) and which are false (F)? Write T or F in the boxes.

1. Mark's hair was cut badly. ☐
2. He had not been to that barber's shop before. ☐
3. It was better than the one he used to go to before. ☐
4. His friend George advised him to choose the barber whose hair looked the worst. ☐

5. Barbers cut each other's hair. ☐

6. The barber whose hair is cut the worst cannot be the worst barber. ☐

B Answer these questions:

1. How did Mark feel when he came out of the barber's shop?
2. What did his friend George do when he saw him?
3. And what did George say?
4. What was Mark's answer?
5. What did George suggest then?
6. And what did Mark answer?
7. What did George say then?
8. Which barber would have the best haircut?

C Choose the right sentences for each picture:

1. a. Mark has cleaned his shoes.
   b. Mark has had his shoes cleaned.
   c. Mark is cleaning his shoes.
   d. Mark is having his shoes cleaned.

2. a. Mark has cleaned his shoes.
   b. Mark has had his shoes cleaned.
   c. Mark is cleaning his shoes.
   d. Mark is having his shoes cleaned.

3. a. Mark has cleaned his shoes.
   b. Mark has had his shoes cleaned.
   c. Mark is cleaning his shoes.
   d. Mark is having his shoes cleaned.

4. a. Mark has cleaned his shoes.
   b. Mark has had his shoes cleaned.
   c. Mark is cleaning his shoes.
   d. Mark is having his shoes cleaned.

17

Mrs Harris's husband died when she was forty-five years old. She had a son, who was eighteen years old at that time.

Mrs Harris was not a widow for very long. She met a nice man who was a few years older than she was, and two years after her first husband had died, she married for the second time. Her son, Peter, was twenty years old then.

Mrs Harris had a nice, quiet wedding in the village church, and after that, they had the usual party at her house for her family and her new husband's, and for some of their friends, but Peter was very late for the party. At last he hurried in, kissed his mother, and said, 'I'm sorry I'm late, Mum, but I've been looking everywhere for a card which says, "To my Mother, for her Wedding," and I haven't been able to find one.'

A Which of these sentences are true (T) and which are false (F)? Write T or F in the boxes.

1. Mrs Harris was twenty-five when Peter was born. □
2. She was forty-seven when she married her second husband. □

Outside the 1 500 headwords: Mum

3. She married him at her house in the village. ☐
4. Peter was in a card shop when his mother's wedding party started. ☐
5. He found the card he wanted in the last shop he went to. ☐
6. He did not find the card he wanted. ☐

B Answer these questions:

1. Why did Mrs Harris marry when she was forty-seven?
2. Who was Peter?
3. How old was he then?
4. What kind of wedding did Mrs Harris have?
5. What happened after the wedding?
6. Why was Peter late?
7. What had he been looking for?
8. Why hadn't he been able to find it?

C Put the correct sentences under the correct pictures:

1. He had been looking in the shops for a card for his mother's wedding.
2. Mrs Harris married for the first time when she was young.
3. Peter arrived very late.
4. She had a son a year later, and she called him Peter.
5. She married him in the village church.
6. Then she met a nice man.
7. Then there was a party at her house.
8. When she was forty-five, her husband died.

37

18

A long time ago, when aeroplanes were not very big or strong yet, all passengers had to be weighed with their luggage, so that planes did not have to carry more than it was safe to carry. Then later, when aeroplanes became bigger and stronger, only the luggage had to be weighed; and now very often, the luggage has to be measured instead of being weighed, because size is more important to the airlines than weight. Aeroplanes are so big and strong now, that they can carry almost any weight.

But before a passenger can travel by Hawaiian Airlines, he or she still has to be weighed. Once when one fat man was asked by the airlines' clerk how much he weighed, he thought for a few seconds and then said to her:

'With or without my clothes?'

'Well, sir,' the girl answered, 'how are you planning to travel?'

A   Which of these sentences are true (T) and which are false (F)? Write T or F in the boxes.

1. Aeroplane passengers were weighed a long time ago.   ☐
2. Later, only the luggage was weighed.   ☐

Outside the 1 500 headwords: airline

3. Even now, aeroplanes are not strong enough to carry heavy weights. ☐
4. Hawaiian Airlines only weigh fat passengers. ☐
5. One fat man did not know whether the airlines' clerk wanted his weight with clothes or without. ☐
6. He wanted to travel without his clothes. ☐

B   Answer these questions:

1. Why did aeroplane passengers have to be weighed a long time ago?
2. Why did they not have to be weighed some years later?
3. What happens to luggage now?
4. Why is it treated in this way?
5. What still happens at Hawaiian Airlines?
6. What did the airlines' clerk there ask one fat man?
7. What did he answer?
8. What did the clerk say then?

C   Do this puzzle:

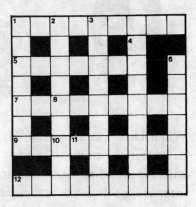

Across:

1. The fat man wanted to travel in an . . . .
5. The . . . why luggage often does not have to be weighed any more is that aeroplanes can now carry more weight than before.
7. The passengers stand . . . line . . . order to give their tickets to the airlines' clerk.
8. This is usually weighed before it is put on a plane.
9.

11. 'What is the . . . of your suitcase?' 'It is 15 kilograms.'
12. The fat man was a . . . on the plane.

Down:

1. The clerk worked for an . . . .
2. 'Was the fat man . . . thinking of travelling without any clothes?' 'No, of course not!'
3. Dug up the ground with a machine.
4. Make plans.
6. Less sour or bitter.
10. We can cook by electricity or . . . .

19

When Dick was six years old, he went and stayed with his grand-parents in the country for a few weeks in the summer. He talked a lot with his grandmother while he was there, and she told him a lot of interesting things about their family which he had not known before. When he came home again to his own parents, he said to his father, 'Is it true that I was born in London, Daddy?'

'Yes, it is, Dick,' his father answered.

'And were you really born in Germany?' Dick asked.

'Yes, that's right,' his father answered. 'I was.'

'And is it true that Mummy was born in Ireland?' Dick continued.

His father said, 'Yes, it is, but why are you asking me all these questions?'

Dick answered, 'Because when Granny told me all those things while I was with her, I couldn't understand how we had all met.'

Outside the 1 500 headwords: Granny

A Which of these sentences are true (T) and which are false (F)? Write T or F in the boxes.

1. Dick and his grandmother talked to each other a lot. ☐
2. Dick already knew a lot about his family. ☐
3. His grandmother told him a lot about it. ☐
4. Dick's parents had been born in the same country. ☐
5. Dick had been born in a different country. ☐
6. Dick had met his parents in Germany. ☐

B Answer these questions:

1. Whom did Dick visit when he was six?
2. How did Dick find out a lot of interesting things about his family?
3. Whom did he talk to about these things when he came home?
4. Where had Dick been born?
5. Where had his father been born?
6. And where had his mother been born?
7. What did his father say when he asked a lot of questions?
8. And what did Dick answer?

C Put *what, which* **or** *who* **in each empty space:**

1. Dick's grandmother told him things . . . he had not known before.
2. She told him . . . he wanted to know.
3. Dick had a father . . . had been born in Germany.
4. It didn't matter . . . Dick asked: his grandmother knew the answer.
5. '. . . a strange thing!' Dick thought. 'We were all born in different places, but we all met.'
6. '. . . of those men is Dick's father?' 'The tallest one.'
7. '. . . is he?' 'He's a teacher.'
8. '. . . is that woman?' 'She's Dick's mother.'

20

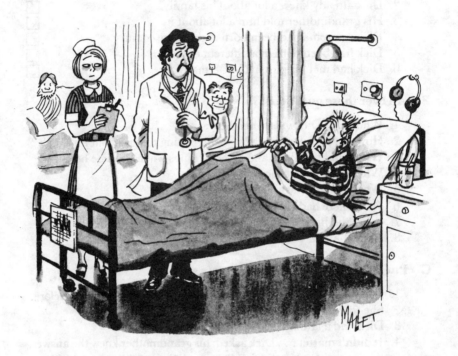

When Dave Perkins was young, he played a lot of games, and he was thin and strong, but when he was forty-five, he began to get fat and slow. He was not able to breathe as well as before, and when he walked rather fast, his heart beat painfully.

He did not do anything about this for a long time, but finally he became anxious and went to see a doctor, and the doctor sent him to hospital. Another young doctor examined him there and said, 'I don't want to mislead you, Mr Perkins. You're very ill, and I believe that you are unlikely to live much longer. Would you like me to arrange for anybody to come and see you before you die?'

Dave thought for a few seconds and then he answered, 'I'd like another doctor to come and see me.'

A   Which of these sentences are true (T) and which are false (F)?
Write T or F in the boxes.

1. Dave was fat and slow until he was forty-five. ☐
2. As soon as Dave had trouble in breathing and walking, he
went to see a doctor. ☐
3. Dave was afraid he was ill. ☐
4. The young doctor thought Dave was going to die soon. ☐
5. He wanted Dave to see another doctor first. ☐
6. Dave did not trust the young doctor. ☐

B   Answer these questions:

1. What was Dave like when he was young?
2. What happened to him when he was forty-five?
3. What did he do about it at first?
4. What did he do later?
5. What did his doctor do?
6. What did the young doctor in the hospital say to Dave?
7. What did he ask him?
8. And what did Dave answer?

C   Put one word in each empty place. You will find all the correct
words in the story on page 42.

When Dave was a very small boy, he had trouble with his lungs.
Sometimes, after running, he was only . . . to . . . very . . . . His mother,
of course, was very . . . about these pains. She took him to the doctor,
and he . . . him carefully and . . . said, 'Well, I . . . that it is . . . to be
anything serious, and that he will grow out of it, but I don't want to . . .
you if I am wrong, so I will . . . for him to go into hospital for tests.' The
tests proved that the doctor was quite right.

21

Joe was one of those people who love the sound of their own voice. He never had anything interesting to say, but he talked and talked and talked, and every story he told reminded him of another one, so that he never stopped for a second to let anybody else say anything.

One evening he was invited to a party by someone whom he had met only a few days before and who did not know him very well yet. They had a good meal, and then they had some music and dancing. Joe danced once with a pretty girl and then suggested that they should sit and talk. He talked and talked and talked, and was just beginning, 'And that reminds me of the time . . . ,' when the girl said, 'The time? Yes, you're quite right!' She looked at her watch quickly and said, 'Look how late it is. I must go.'

A Which of these sentences are true (T) and which are false (F)? Write T or F in the boxes.

1. Joe liked talking very much.
2. People did not enjoy listening to him.
3. He stopped other people saying anything.
4. He was invited to a party by an old friend.
5. Joe wanted to talk instead of dancing.
6. A girl asked Joe to talk instead of dancing.

7. Joe was probably going to say, 'And that reminds me of the time that I was . . . ,' but the girl stopped him. □

8. Joe was probably going to say, 'And that reminds me of the time. It's late. I must go,' but the girl stopped him. □

B   Answer these questions:

1. What kind of person was Joe?
2. What happened whenever he found someone to talk to?
3. What happened one evening?
4. What did Joe and the pretty girl do?
5. What did Joe do then?
6. What was he saying when the girl stopped him?
7. What did she do?
8. And what did she say?

C   Put *forget*, *remember* **or** *remind* **in the first empty place in each of these sentences; and put** *taking* **or** *to take* **in the second empty place in each.**

Mrs Smith always has to . . . her son . . . his coat to school.

Did Mrs Smith's son . . . . . . his coat to school yesterday? Yes, he did.

22

Matthew Hobbs was sixteen years old. He had been at the same school for five years, and he had always been a very bad pupil. He was lazy, he fought with other pupils, he was rude to the teachers, and he did not obey the rules of the school. His headmaster tried to make him work and behave better, but he was never successful—and the worst thing was that, as Matthew grew older, he was a bad influence on the younger boys.

Then at last Matthew left school. He tried to get a job with a big company, and the manager wrote to the headmaster to find out what he could say about Matthew.

The headmaster wanted to be honest, but he also did not want to be too hard, so he wrote, 'If you can get Matthew Hobbs to work for you, you will be very lucky.'

A   Which of these sentences are true (T) and which are false (F)? Write T or F in the boxes.

1. Matthew had come to his school when he was eleven. ☐
2. He was always a good boy. ☐

3. The younger boys learnt good manners from him.
4. Matthew got a job with a big company.
5. His old headmaster got a letter from the manager.
6. The headmaster answered the letter cleverly.

B Answer these questions:

1. How did Matthew behave at school?
2. What did his headmaster do about it?
3. Did he succeed?
4. What made things even worse?
5. What did Matthew do when he left school?
6. What did the manager of the company do?
7. How did the headmaster feel about this?
8. What did he write to the manager?

C Put the right sentences under the right pictures:

1. He did not obey the school rules.
2. He fought with other pupils.
3. He was a bad influence on the younger boys.
4. He was rude to the teachers.
5. Matthew was a lazy boy.
6. The headmaster wrote a clever answer.
7. The manager wrote to his headmaster.
8. Then he left school and tried to get a job in a company.

23

Harry came to his mother one morning while she was having her breakfast, and said to her, 'No one at my school likes me, Mother. The teachers don't, and the children don't. Even the cleaners and the bus drivers hate me.'

'Well, Harry,' his mother answered, 'perhaps you aren't very nice to them. If a *few* people don't like a person, he or she may not be responsible for that; but if a lot of people don't, there's usually something wrong, and that person really needs to change.'

'I'm too old to change,' Harry said. 'I don't want to go to school.'

'Don't be silly, Harry,' his mother said, going towards the garage to get the car out. 'You have to go. You're quite well, and you still have a lot of things to learn. And besides that, you're the headmaster of the school.'

A Which of these sentences are true (T) and which are false (F)? Write T or F in the boxes.

1. Harry was a schoolboy. ☐
2. He liked going to school. ☐
3. His mother wanted him to go to school too. ☐
4. His mother thought he should change, because a lot of people did not like him. ☐

Outside the 1 500 headwords: cleaner

5. She thought he might be too ill to go to school that day. ☐

6. He was the headmaster. ☐

B Answer these questions:

1. What did Harry say to his mother?
2. When did he say this?
3. What did his mother answer?
4. And what did Harry say then?
5. What was his mother's answer?
6. And what did she do while she was saying that?
7. Why did she do this, do you think?
8. What did you think Harry was when you started reading this story?

C Do this puzzle:

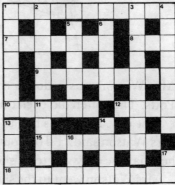

Across:

1. A headmaster is . . . for seeing that everything goes well in his school.
7. Aeroplanes land and take off here.
8. Harry could not . . . why he should go to school.
9. These people clean places.
10. Harry was the headmaster of the . . . .
12. The teachers and the children did not like Harry, and . . . the cleaners and bus drivers hated him.
15. These people teach pupils.
18. These people are the top people in schools.

Down:

1. Harry had several . . . for not wanting to go to school.
2. The pupils probably did not like him because he was . . . with them.
3. These people drive pupils to school.

4.

5. Some teachers are men, and some are . . . .
6. When the headmaster comes into a class, all the pupils . . . up.
11. Harry said to his mother, 'All the people at school . . . me.'
13. All the pupils at that school help . . . other.
14. '. . . afternoon' means 'today, in the afternoon'.
16. If you want to shoot straight, you must . . . your gun carefully.
17. Because.

24

Mrs Watson was a doctor's wife. She had a nice neighbour, Mrs Potts. They often did each other's shopping.

One day, Mrs Potts had to go to Dr Watson because she was ill, so Mrs Watson said, 'I'll do your shopping today, Beryl.' Mrs Potts told her that she only wanted a sheep's kidney.

Mrs Watson went to the shops, and when she came back, she went to Mrs Potts's house, but she was not there, so she went to her own house. She looked in her husband's waiting-room, but Mrs Potts was not there either, so she went into her husband's office. Her husband told her that Mrs Potts had just left him and gone to the lavatory.

Mrs Watson ran out into the crowded waiting-room just in time to catch Mrs Potts. She shouted, 'Here's your kidney!' and ran and gave her the parcel.

A Which of these sentences are true (T) and which are false (F)? Write T or F in the boxes.

1. Mrs Potts lived near Mrs Watson.
2. MrsWatson was ill.
3. Mrs Watson did Mrs Potts's shopping.
4. During this time, Mrs Potts went to the lavatory and then to Dr Watson's office.

Outside the 1 500 headwords: kidney

5. Mrs Watson stopped Mrs Potts as she was leaving. ☐

6. Dr Watson had cut Mrs Potts's kidney out. ☐

B Answer these questions:

1. What work did Mrs Watson's husband do?
2. Who was Mrs Potts?
3. How did she and Mrs Watson help each other?
4. Why did Mrs Watson offer to do Mrs Potts's shopping one day?
5. What did Mrs Potts ask her to get?
6. Where did Mrs Watson look for Mrs Potts when she came back?
7. Where was Mrs Potts?
8. What did Mrs Watson shout to her when she found her at last?

C Write the sentences for each picture. Choose the correct words.

1. Mrs Potts came in { seeing / to see } the doctor.

2. She came in { laughing. / to laugh. }

3. She said, 'I can't help { laughing. / to laugh. } I've just heard a good joke.'

4. Dr Watson's nurse helped her { to walk. / walking. }

5. The doctor said, 'Are you willing { to wait / waiting } a few minutes? This machine needs { mending.' / to mend.' }

6. She answered, 'No, I don't mind { to wait. / waiting. } You don't need { hurrying.' / to hurry.' }

25

Jim was intelligent, but he hated hard work. He said, 'You work hard, and earn a lot of money, and then the government takes most of it. I want easy work that gives me lots of money and that the government doesn't know about.'

So he became a thief—but *he* did not do the stealing: he got others to do it. They were much less intelligent than he was, so he arranged everything and told them what to do.

One day they were looking for rich families to rob, and Jim sent one of them to a large beautiful house just outside the town.

It was evening, and when the man looked through one of the windows, he saw a young man and a girl playing a duet on a piano.

When he went back to Jim, he said, 'That family can't have much money. Two people were playing on the same piano there.'

Outside the 1 500 headwords: duet, rob

A Which of these sentences are true (T) and which are false (F)? Write T or F in the boxes.

1. Jim was clever, but lazy. ☐
2. He didn't like paying taxes. ☐
3. He always used clever people to steal for him. ☐
4. They tried to find rich families. ☐
5. One of his men played a duet on a piano with a girl. ☐
6. The girl's family was poor. ☐

B Answer these questions:

1. Why did Jim become a thief?
2. How did he steal things?
3. What was *his* job in this?
4. Why was he good at it?
5. What did he send one of his men to do one evening?
6. What did the man see?
7. What did he say to Jim?
8. What mistake did he make?

C *Opposites:* **Find words in the story on page 52 which mean about the opposite of:**

1. difficult
2. lazy
3. little
4. more
5. old
6. poor
7. small
8. spend
9. stupid
10. ugly

26

Fred sometimes liked to go to a bar to have a drink before he went home after work. There were some tables and chairs in the bar, but it was too early for most people when Fred was there, so he seldom found anyone to talk to.

Then one evening he went into the bar and saw a man playing draughts at a table, but he could not see anyone in the chair opposite him. He went nearer to look, and was very surprised to see that the man was playing against a dog. When it had to move one of its draughts, it stood on its back legs on the chair.

Fred watched while the two played their game, and when the dog lost, Fred went up to its owner and said, 'I've never seen such a clever dog before.'

'Well,' answered the other man, 'he isn't really very clever. I always win.'

A Which of these sentences are true (T) and which are false (F)? Write T or F in the boxes.

1. Fred always had his drink at home. ☐
2. He talked to a lot of people in a bar. ☐

Outside the 1 500 headwords: draughts

3. A man was playing draughts with a dog in the bar one evening.
4. The dog moved the draughts itself.
5. Fred was very surprised.
6. The dog sometimes won the game.

☐
☐
☐
☐

B   Answer these questions:

1. Where did Fred sometimes go after work?
2. Why did he seldom find anyone to talk to there?
3. What did he see one evening?
4. Why was he very surprised when he went nearer?
5. How did the dog manage to play?
6. Who won?
7. What did Fred say then?
8. What did the dog's owner answer?

C   Put the right sentences under the right pictures:

1. A man was playing draughts at a table.
2. Fred could not see anyone playing against him.
3. Fred went into his usual bar.
4. He sat down at a table.
5. He saw a dog sitting in the chair opposite the man.
6. He went nearer.
7. The bar was almost empty.
8. When the dog wanted to move a draught, it stood on its back legs on the chair.

27

Henry was from the United States and he had come to London for a holiday.

One day he was not feeling well, so he went to the clerk at the desk of his hotel and said, 'I want to see a doctor. Can you give me the name of a good one?'

The clerk looked in a book and then said, 'Dr Kenneth Grey, 61010.'

Henry said, 'Thank you very much. Is he expensive?'

'Well,' the clerk answered, 'he always charges his patients two pounds for their first visit to him, and £1.50 for later visits.'

Henry decided to save 50p, so when he went to see the doctor, he said, 'I've come again, doctor.'

For a few seconds the doctor looked at his face carefully without saying anything. Then he nodded and said, 'Oh, yes.' He examined him and then said, 'Everything's going as it should do. Just continue with the medicine I gave you last time.'

Outside the 1 500 headwords: charge (*v.*)

A **Which of these sentences are true (T) and which are false (F)? Write T or F in the boxes.**

1. Henry wanted the clerk at the hotel to send a good doctor to his room. □
2. The clerk gave him the name and address of a doctor. □
3. Henry wanted to know how much it cost to go to him. □
4. The first visit to the doctor cost less than later visits. □
5. Henry tried to make the doctor believe that he had been to him before. □
6. The doctor knew that he had not seen Henry before. □

B **Answer these questions:**

1. Why did Henry have to ask someone else for the name of a doctor?
2. What did the clerk do?
3. What did Henry ask him then?
4. And what did the clerk answer?
5. What did Henry decide?
6. What did he do?
7. What did he say to the doctor?
8. And what was the doctor's answer?

C **Put one word in each empty place. You will find all the correct words in the story on page 56.**

Dr Brown is a kind man. He left England to work in a foreign country when he was 25. Some of his . . . are quite poor, and he . . . them very little. And when they need . . . medicines, he sometimes even pays for them himself. One day a . . . who worked in a small office brought him his son. He was very ill, and he knew that only very expensive medicines could . . . him from dying. Dr Brown . . . the boy carefully. 'Well,' the father said, 'what have you found, doctor? Will he be all right?' The doctor . . . without looking at him. He thought for a minute and then said, 'Yes, he'll be all right. I'm going to give you some medicine for him. He must . . . taking it for a month. We don't want him to die, do we?'

28

Mrs Jenkins was the owner of a small restaurant in Southampton. Southampton is a big port. Mrs Jenkins had two young waitresses and a cook to help her.

One day a sailor came into the restaurant, sat down at one of the tables, ordered what he wanted from the waitress and then got up and left again after a few minutes. The owner of the restaurant was surprised when she saw this, so she called the waitress and asked her why the man had left before having his meal.

'Well,' the waitress answered, 'he asked for some of our fried rabbit, and when I went out into the kitchen to order it from the cook, the cat was just on the other side of the door and I stepped on its tail by mistake. It made a terrible noise, of course, and then the man got up from his table and went out very quickly.'

A Which of these sentences are true (T) and which are false (F)? Write T or F in the boxes.

1. Mrs Jenkins's restaurant was very big. ☐
2. A sailor came in, but he did not like the waitress, so he went out again. ☐
3. Mrs Jenkins was surprised when the sailor left. ☐

4. The sailor ordered rabbit for his meal.
5. The cat made a noise because its tail hurt.
6. The restaurant gave people cat's meat instead of rabbit's.

B Answer these questions:

1. What was Mrs Jenkins's job?
2. Who did she have working for her?
3. What did the sailor do?
4. Why was Mrs Jenkins surprised?
5. What did she do then?
6. What did she ask the waitress?
7. And what did the waitress answer?
8. What had the sailor thought?

C Choose the correct sentence for each picture:

1. The sailor arrived $\begin{Bmatrix} \text{much} \\ \text{too} \\ \text{very} \end{Bmatrix}$ late,

   but he was not $\begin{Bmatrix} \text{much} \\ \text{too} \\ \text{very} \end{Bmatrix}$ late to get

   some lunch.

2. The waitress was $\begin{Bmatrix} \text{much} \\ \text{too} \\ \text{very} \end{Bmatrix}$

   surprised when the sailor left, but

   Mrs Jenkins was $\begin{Bmatrix} \text{much} \\ \text{too} \\ \text{very} \end{Bmatrix}$ more

   surprised.

3. The sailor could run $\begin{Bmatrix} \text{much} \\ \text{too} \\ \text{very} \end{Bmatrix}$

   fast, but his friend could run

   $\begin{Bmatrix} \text{much} \\ \text{too} \\ \text{very} \end{Bmatrix}$ faster.

29

There is a prison in Iceland which allows its prisoners to go out without any guards to work every day. They work on the farms near the prison during the day, and come back to have their evening meal and to sleep every evening. Before they are allowed to go out like this, they have to promise to come back every evening. If they do not promise this, they are not let out.

One night one of the prisoners was invited to have a meal and a drink with the family of the farmer he was working for, so he came back to the prison very late. He had to knock at the gate several times before the guard came to let him in.

The guard did not like being disturbed at this time, so he said to the prisoner angrily, 'If you come back so late again, I won't let you in.'

Outside the 1 500 headwords: guard (*n.*)

**A   Which of these sentences are true (T) and which are false (F)?
Write T or F in the boxes.**

1. The guards in the prison in Iceland were on the farms
   with the prisoners during the day. ☐
2. The prisoners had to have their evening meal on the farms. ☐
3. They spent the night in the prison. ☐
4. One prisoner had his meal on a farm one evening. ☐
5. The guard did not like opening the gate late at night
   because he was afraid. ☐
6. He did not let the prisoner in. ☐

B   Answer these questions:

1. In what way is the prison in this story different from most others?
2. What work do the prisoners do?
3. What do they have to do in order to be allowed to work outside?
4. What happens if they do not do this?
5. Why was one prisoner very late one night?
6. What did he have to do to get into the prison again?
7. How did the guard feel about this?
8. What did he threaten to do if the prisoner was late again?

C   Put *it, not* **or** *so* **in each empty place, but only if one of these is
needed:**

1. 'Did all the prisoners promise to come back every evening?' 'Yes, I
   think . . . .'
2. 'Did they always come back?' 'No, I expect . . . .'
3. 'Did the prisoners work really hard on the farms?' 'I wonder . . . .'
4. 'Did the farmer who invited the prisoner like him?' 'Yes, I suppose
   . . . .'
5. 'Do you think the prisoner who was late ever came late again?' 'I
   doubt . . . .'
6. 'Did the guards ever lock a prisoner out?' 'No, I hope . . . .'
7. 'I think that was a nice prison.' 'I agree . . . .'
8. 'We have prisons like that in Britain too.' 'I don't believe
   . . . !'

Peter was 10 years old, and he was having painting lessons every week at a small private class.

During the Christmas holidays, he had a party at his home, and he wanted to invite one of the other students, but he only knew her name — Celia Poe. He did not know her address or her telephone number.

Peter's mother looked in the telephone book and said, 'Well, there are only four Poes here, so I'll telephone each of them and ask whether they have a daughter who has painting lessons.'

She telephoned the first one, and the telephone rang for rather a long time before a woman answered. Peter's mother said, 'Excuse me. Is that the Mrs Poe who has a daughter who takes painting lessons?'

'No, it isn't,' the woman answered. 'This is the Mrs Poe who had to get out of her bath to answer the telephone!'

A   Which of these sentences are true (T) and which are false (F)? Write T or F in the boxes.

1. Peter studied painting with a lot of other children.
2. One of the other students was called Celia.
3. There were a lot of Poes in the telephone book.
4. The first one that Peter's mother telephoned was Celia's mother.
5. Peter's mother spoke to Mrs Poe politely.
6. The woman was in her bath when the telephone rang.

☐
☐
☐

☐
☐
☐

B   Answer these questions:

1. How old was Peter?
2. Where did he study painting?
3. Why did he want to telephone Celia?
4. Why was it not easy to do this?
5. How did his mother plan to help him?
6. What did she say to the first woman she telephoned?
7. And what was the woman's answer?
8. How did the woman feel, do you think?

C   Do this puzzle:

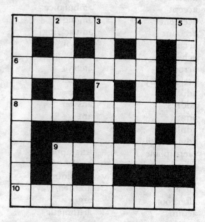

Across:

1. This tells you when you have to go to each class.
6. Peter was having these every week.
8. 'Was Peter studying painting in a public class?' 'No, he was studying it . . . .'
9. 'What did Peter do in his class?' 'He . . . pictures.'
10. All people.

Down:

1. A woman had to get out of her bath to answer this.
2. Have to.
3. Also.
4. Having the most work to do.

5. 'Did Peter like his painting lessons?' 'Yes, he . . . them very much.'
7. 'Did Peter find Celia's telephone number . . . ?' 'No, it was very difficult.'
9. Peter's friend was called Celia . . . .

APPENDIX

A 1 500-word Vocabulary

Note: This vocabulary does not contain numerals, names of the days of the week, names of the months, or proper nouns and adjectives. Not all the cases of nouns and pronouns are given (e.g. *boy* stands for *boy—boy's—boys—boys'*; *I* stands for *I—me—my—mine*); nor are all parts of verbs given (e.g. *swim* stands for *swim—swims—swam—swum—swimming*). Comparatives and superlatives of adjectives and adverbs are also not given.

The abbreviation *a.* means adjective and/or adverb; *conj.* means conjunction; *n.* means noun; *prep.* means preposition; and *v.* means verb.

(Words outside the list are printed at the bottom of the pages on which they are used—for example, *relax*, on page 6.)

a[n]	along	ask	be
able/ability	already	asleep	beach
about	also	at	beak
above	[al]though	attack	bean
abroad	always	audience	bear (*n.*)
absent	a.m.	aunt	bear (*v.*)
accept	ambulance	autumn	beard
accident	among	avoid	beat (*v.*)
account	amuse[/ing]	awake	beautiful
accuse	anchor	away	because
ache	and	axe	become
across	angry		bed[room]
act[or/ress]	animal	baby	bee
add	ankle	back (*a.*)	beer
address	answer	back (*n.*)	before
admit	ant	bad (worse,	beg[gar]
adult	anxious/iety	worst)	begin[ning]
advice/advise	any	bag	behave
[aero]plane	[dis]appear	bake	behind
afford	apple	ball	believe
afraid	appointment	balloon	bell
after	arch[ed/way]	banana	belong
afternoon	argue	band	below
again	arithmetic	bandage	belt
against	arm	bank	bench
ago	army	bar	bend
[dis]agree	around	barber	beside
aim	arrange[ment]	bargain	besides
air[force/mail/	arrest	bark	between
port]	arrive[/al]	basin	bicycle
algebra	article	basket	big
all	artist[ic]	bath[room]	bill
allow[ance]	as	bathe	bird
almost	ash[tray]	battery	birthday
alone	ashamed	battle	biscuit

bite
bitter
black
blackboard
blame
blanket
blind
blood
blouse
blow
blue
boast
boat
body (and
  -*body*, e.g. in
  anybody)
boil (*v.*)
bold
bomb
bone
book[-case]
boot
born
borrow
both
bottle
bottom
bowl (*n.*)
box (*n.*)
boy
bracelet
branch
brass
brave
bread
break
breakfast
breathe
bribe
brick
bridge
bright
bring
broadcast
broken
brother
brown
bruise
brush
bucket
build[ing]
bullet
bunch
burn
burst
bus

bush
business[man]
busy
but
butter[-dish]
butterfly
button
buy
by

cabbage
cage
cake
call
calm
camera
camp
can (*n.*)
can (*v.*)
canal
candle
cap
capital
captain
car
card
cardboard
care
careful[/less]
carpet
carriage
carry
cart
case
castle
cat
catch
cause
cave
ceiling
celebrate
cent
centimetre
ceremony
certain
chain
chair
chalk
chance
change
charcoal
cheap
cheat
cheek
cheese
chemist

chest
chicken
child
chimney
chin
chocolate
choose
Christmas
church
cigarette
cinema
circle
circus
city
class[room]
clean
clear
clerk
clever
cliff
climate
climb
clock
close (*a.*)
close[d]
cloth
clothes
cloud[y]
club
coal[-mine]
coat
cock
coffee[-pot]
cold
collar
collect
college
colour
column
comb
come
[un]comfortable
[un]common
company
complain
composition
confess
confused
congratulate
continue[/al]
cook[ing]
cool
copy
cork[screw]
corn
corner

correct
cost
cotton[-wool]
cough
count (*v.*)
country
course
cousin
cover[ed]
cow
crack[ed]
crawl
crop
cross (*n.*)
cross (*v.*)
crowd[ed]
cry
cup
cupboard
cure
curious
curtain
custom
cut
cycle (*v.*)

dad[dy]
damage[d]
damp
dance[-band]
danger[ous]
dare
dark
date
daughter
day/daily
dead
deaf
dear
decide/decision
deep
deer
degree
delighted
dentist
department
depend
describe
desert (*n.*)
desk
destroy
dictionary
die
different
difficult
dig

dining[-room,
-hall]
dinner
dirty
disappointed
discover
dish
disturb
ditch
dive
divide
do
doctor (Dr)
dog
dollar
donkey
door
double
doubt[ful]
down
dozen
draw[ing]
drawer
dream
dress
drink
drive[r]
drop (n.)
drop (v.)
drown
drum
drunk
dry
duck
dull
dumb
during
duster
dust[y]

each
eager
ear[-ring]
early
earn
earth
east[ern]
Easter
easy
eat
edge
egg
either
electric[ity]
elephant
else

empty
end
enemy
engine
enjoy
enough
envelope
envy
equal
escape
even
evening
ever (and -ever,
e.g. in whoever)
every[where]
exact
examine[/ation/
er]
except
excited
excuse
exercise
expect
expensive
explain/
explanation
explode
explore[r]
eye

face[-powder]
factory
fade
fail
faint
faithfully
fall
false
family
famous
fan
far
farm[er]
fast
fat
father
feather
feed
feel[ing]
fence
fever
few
field
fierce
fight
fill

film
finally
find
fine (a.)
finger
finish[ed]
fire[place]
first
fish[erman/ing-
rod]
flag
flat (a.)
flat (n.)
float
flood
floor
flour
flower
fly (n.)
fly (v.)
fog[gy]
fold
follow
fond
food
foolish
foot[ball]
for
foreign[er]
forest
forget
forgive
fork
forward[s]
frame
free
freeze
frequent (a.)
fresh
friend
frighten[ed]
from
front
fruit
fry
full
fun[ny]
furniture
further[/est]
future

game
garage
garden
gas
gate

gay
general (a.)
generous
gentleman
geography
geometry
get
girl
give
glad
glass[es]
glue
go
goal
goat
God
gold[-mine]
good (better,
best)
goodbye
government
gram
grand- (e.g. in
grandfather)
grape
grass
green
greet
grey
grill
ground
group
grow
growl
guess
guest
guide[-book]
gun

hair
half [penny]
hall
hammer
hand
handkerchief
handle
handsome
hang
happen
happy
hard
hardly
harvest[-time]
hat
hate
have

he
headmaster/
  mistress
hear
heart
heavy
help
hen
here
hide (v.)
high
hill
hire (v.)
history
hit
hobby
hold
hole
holiday
hollow
home[work]
[dis]honest
honey
hook
hooray
hope[ful/less]
horn
horse[back/
  man/shoe]
hospital
host[ess]
hot/heat[ing]
hotel
hour[ly/-hand]
house
how
hullo
hungry
hunt[er]
hurry
hurt
husband
hut

I
ice[-cream]
if
ill[ness]
imagine
important
in[to]
influence
[in]flu[enza]
injection
ink

-in-law (e.g.
  son-in-law)
insect
inside
instead
intelligent
intend[/tion]
interest[ed/ing]
introduce[/
  tion]
invent[ion/or]
invite[/ation]
iron
island
it

jam[-dish/jar]
jar
jealous
jewellery
job
join
joke
journalist
journey
judge
jug
jump
just

keep
key
kick
kill
kilo[gram]
kilometre
kind (a.)
kind (n.)
king
kiss
kitchen
kite
knee[l]
knife
knock
know

ladder
lady
lake
lamp
land
language
large
last (a. & n.)
late

lately
laugh
lavatory
lay
lazy
lead[er]
  (mislead)
leaf
leak
lean (v.)
learn
least
leather
leave
lecture[r]
left[-hand]
leg
lend
less
lesson
let
letter
library[/ian]
lid
lie (n. & v.)
lie (v.)
lift
light (a.)
light (n. & v.)
like (a.)
like (v.)
[un]likely
limit
line
lion
lip
list
listen[er]
litre
little
live (v.)
living-room
[un]load
loaf
local
[un] lock[ed]
long (a.)
look
loose
lose (lost)
lot
loud
love
low
lucky
luggage

lump
lunch
lung

machine
mad
madam
magazine
main
make
man
manage[r]
manners
many
map
marbles
march
mark
market[-place]
marry[/iage/ied]
mat
match[box]
mathematics
matter
may (v.)
mayor
meal
mean (v.)
measure
meat
medicine
meet[ing]
melt
member
mend
merchant
merry
message[/enger]
metal
metre
midday
middle
midnight
milk[-bottle/
  -jug]
millimetre
mind
mine[r]
minister
minute[-hand]
mirror
miss (v.)
Miss
mistake
mix
model

modern
moment
money
monkey
month[ly]
moon
more
morning
mosque
mosquito
most
mother
motor[-car/
 -cycle]
mountain
mouse[-trap]
moustache
mouth
move
Mr[s]
much
mud[dy]
multiply
mum[my]
music
must
mysterious

nail
name
narrow
nasty
navy
near
nearly
necessary
neck
necklace
need
needle
neighbour
neither
nephew
nest
net
never
new
news[paper]
next
nice
niece
night[ly]
no
nod
noise/noisy
none

nor
north[ern]
nose
not
notebook
notice[-board]
now
nuisance
number
nurse
nut

oar
obey[/dient]
occasional
o'clock
of
off
offer
office
officer
often
oh
oil
old
on
once
one (and -one,
 e.g. in anyone)
only
open
operation
opposite
or
orange
order
ordinary
ornament
other
ought
out
outside
oven
over[coat]
owe
own[er]

pack[age]
packet
page
pain[ful]
paint[er]
pair
pan
paper
parcel

pardon
parent
park
part
party
pass
passenger
passport
past
path
patient (a.)
patient (n.)
pay
pen
pencil[-box]
penny
people
perhaps
permission
person
persuade
petrol
photograph
physics
piano
pick
picnic
picture
piece
pig
pile
pillow
pin
pink
pipe
pity
place
plan
plant
plate
play[ground]
[un]pleasant
please[d]
plenty
plough
p.m.
pocket[-book]
poem
point (n.)
point (v.)
poisonous
police[man]
polite
pond
pool
poor

port
porter
position
[im]possible
post[card/man/office]
post (n.)
pot
potato
pound
pour
powder
practise
praise
pray
prefer
prepare
present (a.)
present (n.)
president
press (v.)
pretend
pretty
prevent
price
prime minister
prince[ss]
prison[er]
private
prize
probable
produce
programme
promise
pronounce
proof/prove
proud
public
pull
pump
punctual
punish
pupil
pure
purple
purpose
push
put
puzzle[/ing]

quarrel
quarter
queen
question[-mark]
quick
quiet
quite

rabbit
race
racket
radio
rail[ing/
  way]
rain[y/coat]
rare
rat
rather
razor
reach
read
ready[-made]
real
realize
reason
recent
recite
recognize
record[-player]
red
refrigerator
refuse (v.)
[ir]regular
relative (n.)
remember
remind
rent
repeat
republic
resign
responsible
rest
restaurant
result
retire
return
ribbon
rice
rich
rid
ride
right[-hand]
ring (n.)
ring (v.)
ripe
river
road
roar
rock
rod
roll
roof
room
root

rope
rose
rotten
rough
round
row (n. + v.)
rub
rubber
rubbish
rude
rug
rule (n.)
ruler
run
rust[y]

sack
sad
safe
sail
sailor
salary
salt[y]
same
sand[y]
sandwich
[dis]satisfied
sauce
saucer
sausage
save
saw
say
scales
scenery
school[-time]
scissors
scold
score
scout
scratch
screw[driver]
  (unscrew)
sea[-shell/side]
season
seat
second (n.)
secret
see
seed
seem
seldom
-self/selves
[un]selfish
sell
send

sentence
separate
serious
servant
several
sew[ing]
shade[/y]
shadow
shake
shall
shallow
shape
share
sharp
shave
she
shed
sheep
sheet
shelf
shell
shine
ship
shirt
shoe[maker]
shoot
shop[keeper]
shore
short
shorts
shoulder
shout
show
shut
shy
sick
side
sign[post]
signal
signature
silk
silly
silver
since
sincere
sing[er]
single
sink
sir
sister
sit
size
skin
skirt
sky
sleep[y]

slice
slide
slip[pery]
slope[/ing]
slow
small
smell
smile
smoke[/ing-
  carriage]
smooth
snake
snow
so
soap
sock
soft
soldier
solid
some
sometimes
son
song[-book]
soon
sore
sorry
sound (n. & v.)
soup
sour
south[ern]
sow
spade
spare
speak
spell[ing]
spend
spill
spit
splash
spoil
spoon[ful]
sport
spread
spring[time]
square
squat
stage
stain
stairs/staircase
  (also -stairs,
  e.g. in upstairs)
stale
stamp
stand
star
start

69

station
stay
steal
steam[er/boat/
  -engine/ship]
steel
steep
steer[ing-wheel]
step
stick (n.)
stick[y]
sticking-plaster
stiff
still
sting
stocking
stomach
stone
stop
store[-house/
  keeper/room]
storm[y]
story
stove
straight
strange[r]
straw
stream
street
stretch
strict
string
strong
student
study
stuff
stupid
submarine
succeed[/ess
  /ful]
such
suck
sudden
sugar[-bowl]
suggest[ion]
suit[case]
suit (v.)
sum
summer[time]
sun[burnt/ny/
  rise/set/shine]
supper
support
suppose
sure
surprised[/ing]

surround[ing[s]]
swallow (v.)
sweat
sweep
sweet
swim[mer]
swing[ing]
switch
sword

table
tablet
tail
tailor
take
talk
tall
tame
tank
tap
taste
taxi
tea[pot]
teach[er]
team
tear (v.)
telegram
telephone
television
tell
temperature
temple
tennis
tent
term
terrible
test
than
thank[ful/s]
that/those
that (conj.)
the
theatre
then
there
thermometer
they
thick
thief
thin
thing (also
  -thing, e.g. in
  nothing)
think
thirsty

this/these
thorn[y]
thread
threaten
throat
through
throw
thumb
thunder
ticket
tidy
tie (n. and v.)
  (untie)
tiger
tight
till (prep.)
time[table]
tin[ned]
tip
tired[/ing]
title
to
tobacco
today
toe
together
tomorrow
tongue
tonight
tonne
too
tool
tooth[paste]
top
torch
total
touch
tough
towards
towel
tower
town
toy
traffic
train (n.)
trap
travel[ler]
tray
treat
tree
tremble
trip
trouble
trousers
truck
true[/thful]

trumpet
trunk
trust
try
tune
tunnel
turn[ing]
twice
type[writer]
  (typist)
tyre

ugly
umbrella
uncle
under
understand
university
unless
until
up[on]
urgent
use
used to
useful[/less]
usually

valley
value[/able]
van
various
vase
vegetable
very
view
village
violin
visit[or]
voice
volcano
volley-ball
voyage

wages
waist[coat]
wait
waiter[/tress]
wake
walk[ing-stick]
wall
want
war
-wards (e.g. in
  backwards)
warm
warn

wash[ing/
  house]
waste
watch (*n.*)
watch (*v.*)
water[-bottle/
  fall/-jug/
  -pipe]
wave
way
we
weak
wear
weather
wedding
week[end/ly]
weigh
welcome
well (*a.*)
west[ern]
wet

what
wheel
when[ever]
where (also
  -where, e.g. in
  somewhere)
whether
which
while
whisper
whistle
white
who
whole
why
wide
widow[er]
wife
wild
will (*v.*)

[un]willing
win
wind[y]
window
wine
wing
winter[time]
wipe
wire
[un]wise
wish
with[out]
woman
wonder[ful]
wood[en/land/
  work]
wool[len]
word
work[er]
world

worm
worry[/ied/ing]
worth
wound
wrap
wrist[watch]
write
wrong

yard
year[ly]
yellow
yes
yesterday
yet
you
young

zero
zoo

저자소개

L. A. Hill 박사는 ELT(English Language Teaching)
교재의 저술가로서 그리고 영어 교육계의 세계적인
권위자로 널리 알려진 분으로 그의 저서에는 다음과 같은
것들이 있다.
Stories for Reproduction 1 (전 4 권), Stories for
Reproduction 2 (전 4 권), Stories for Reproduction:
American Series (전 3 권), Steps to Understanding
(전 4 권), Word Power 1500/3000/4500 (전 3 권),
English through Cartoons (전 2 권), Elementary &
Intermediate Composition Pieces (전 2 권), Elementary &
Intermediate Comprehension Pieces (전 2 권),
Intermediate Comprehension Topics, Oxford Graded
Readers (전 4 권), Writing for a Purpose, Note-taking
Practice, A Guide to Correct English & Exercises
(전 2 권), Prepositions & Adverbial Particles &
Exercises (전 2 권), Contextualized Vocabulary Tests
(전 4 권), Crossword Puzzle Book (전 4 권).

Intermediate Steps to Understanding 3

1985년 2월 5일 인쇄
1985년 2월 12일 발행

지은이 L. A. HILL
펴낸이 李 瀅 載
펴낸곳 外國語研修社

판권
본사
소유

 (株)外國語研修社
Foreign Language Limited
서울·永登浦區 汝矣島洞 35-2 白象빌딩 1006호
☎780-3644 · 785-0919 · 1749 FAX. 780-2817
₩ 8,000

※ 이 책은 옥스포드대학 출판부와의 계약에 의하여 外國語研修社
가 한국내 독점출판권을 가지고 있으므로 外國語研修社의 서
면에 의한 사전 승락 없이는 어떠한 방법으로도 그 일부 또는
전부의 복사 또는 전재를 금합니다.
This edition is published by arrangement with Oxford
University Press. Neither this book nor any part therof may
be reproduced by any process whatsoever without the written
permission of Foreign Language Limited and Oxford
University Press.

Oxford 대학출판부/외국어연수사간 (한국내 판권 : 외국어연수사에서 보유)
ESL/EFL 교재 저술의 세계적 권위 L.H.Hill 박사의 명저

Stories for Reproduction Series 1~4
이야기의 재현(再現)을 통해 배우는 영어 1~4집

■ 흥미진진한 이야기를 읽거나 듣고 말과 글로 다시 표현해 보는 연습을 통해 표현력(作文·會話)·이해력(讀解·聽解)을 획기적으로 향상시키는 교재

- 이미 40여권의 ESL/EFL(English as a Second/Foreign Language) 교재 저술로 세계적 명성을 떨치고 있는 Leslie A. Hill 박사가 그의 오랜 연구와 교육자로서의 경험을 토대로 최근에 집대성한 영어학습교재의 결정판.

- Hill 박사 특유의 Contextualized Approach(문맥적 접근법)에 토대를 둔 다양한 Oral /Written Reproduction Questions & Exercises (구두 / 필기재현연습)로 표현력과 이해력의 획기적 향상.

- A. S. Hornby 의 Guide to Patterns & Usage in English(25 구문 유형)에 토대를 두고 단어와 구문의 난이도에 따라 상용 기본단어를 4 단계(입문, 초급, 중급, 상급)로 나누어 익히고 활용시키는 교재 총서.

- 영어 실력이 약한 경우는 기초실력 재확립용으로, 어휘력·문법실력이 앞선 경우는 속독력·청해력·작문력·회화력 향상용으로 쓸 수 있는 교재.

- 교실수업, 자습 양용으로 쓸 수 있으며 자습의 경우를 위해 상세하고 친절한 주석과 해답이 담긴 Study Guide와 Answer Key를 마련.

■ 대학입시·취직시험·각종고시·TOFEL 등 각종 영어 시험 준비용으로 최적.

제 1 집　Introductory, Elementary, Intermediate Advanced Stories for Reproduction 1
　　　　전 4권　Textbook＋Study Guide＋Cassette Pack.

제 2 집　Introductory, Elementary, Intermediate, Advanced Stories for Reproduction 2
　　　　전 4권　Textbook＋Answer Key＋Cassette Pack.

제 3 집　Introductory, Elementary, Intermediate, Advanced Steps to Understanding
　　　　전 4권　Textbook＋Answer Key＋Cassette Pack.

제 4 집　Elementary, Intermediate, Advanced Stories for Reproduction, American
　　　　Series 전 3권　Textbook＋Answer Key＋Cassette Pack.

Oxford대학출판부/외국어연수사 간(한국내 판권보유 : 외국어연수사)

영어단어연습문제 및 해답 각 3권
Word Power 1500/3000/4500 (한국판)
Vocabulary Tests & Exercises in American English

■EFL/ESL (English as a Foreign/Second Language)교사 및 저술가로서 세계적 권위 Leslie A. Hill 박사의 최신의 명저.

■문맥적 시험 및 연습(Contextualized Tests & Exercises)을 통한 어휘·작문·독해· 회화 실력의 동시 양성.

■대입고사·취직시험·각종 고시·TOEFL 등 각종 시험 준비에 최적

●Structure Words의 철저한 시험/연습으로 구문력(構文力) 양성.

●Picture/Passage의 문맥적 연습(단어의 문맥적 추리→해답과 대조→기억→활용) 으로 독해력(讀解力) 향상.

●Synonyms (유어), Oppoites (반의어), Derivatives (파생어)의 연습으로 풍부한 표현력 (작문력, 회화력) 양성.

●Words in Sentences 연습으로 Content Words 및 Structure Words의 활용 능력 향상.

●Prepositions 및 Adverbial Particles (구동사 : 句動詞)연습으로 미국 영어 숙어 (熟 語)의 정확한 용법 체득.

발상과 어원에 따라 쉽게 풀어쓴
영어숙어
Kosofsky 교수의 최신간 영어학습서

저자 : David Kosofsky
The University of Maryland에서 서양사, Brandeis University에서 비교역사학 전공
미·일·말레이지아에서 영어를 가르쳤고 1982년 내한 6년간 서강대학교 영어교육연구소에서 영어학습
교재를 연구 개발했다. 현재 외국어대학교 영어과 교수.

──── 특색 ────

●사람의 신체와 관련돼 변화무쌍하게 파생하는 숙어표현을 총망라했습니다.

●재미있는 대화와 해설을 보며 숙어의 발상과 어원에 흥미롭게 접근할 수 있습니다.

●대역이 있어 영어가 약한 사람도 누구나 즐겨가며 공부할 수 있습니다.

전국의 유명 서점에 있습니다. *432쪽/값 9,500원

(주)외국어 연수사

Enguiries to : FOREIGN LANGUAGE LTD·☎ 785-0919, 1749 여의도 백상빌딩 10층

만 화 영 어

만화를 즐기며 연마하는 **영어**회화 · 작문교재

English through Cartoons

Dialogues, Stories & Questions

유우머와 **기지**가 넘치는 **만화**를 즐기면서

(A)**대화**(Dialogues)를 읽거나 테이프를 듣고 영어 특유의
　유우머 감각을 몸에 익히며

(B)만화를 해설하는 **이야기**(Stories)를 공란을 메우면서 완성하는
　연습을 통해 **작문력**을 기르고

C)만화내용의 **질의 응답**을 통해 격조 높은 영어 **회화력**을
　양성하는 영작문 · 회화 연습 교재의 결정판 /

● EFL／ESL(English as a Foreign／Second Language)교재 저술의 세계적 권위
Leslie A. Hill 박사와　세계적인 만화가 **D. Mallet** 의 최신 역작.

● 폭소와 홍소를 자아내게 하면서도 깊은 뜻을 담은 만화와 대화는 학습상의 긴장을
덜어 주며 Stories 의 공란을 추리하여 완성토록 유도하는 연습문제와 내용 파악
질의문은 영어의 회화력 · 청취력 · 작문력 · 독해력을 획기적으로 연마 · 향상.

● 학습부담을 줄이고 능률을 최대한으로 올리기 위하여 친절하고 자세한 해설과 예문이
풍부하게 수록된 **Study Guide**를 따로 마련.

주석 · 증보판

PRACTICE WITH IDIOMS
영어 숙어 연습

Ronald E. Fear 원저
李 澄 載 譯編

〈특 장〉

● 영어 숙어의 뜻과 구문 지식을 체계적으로 습득하기 위한 중-상급 수준의 영어 학습 교재이다.

● 복잡 다단한 영어 숙어를 16종의 구문 유형으로 분류하고 각 유형에 속하는 숙어로 연습문제를 구성하여 그것들을 문맥적으로 이해하는 과정에 학습자를 참여시킨 다음 숙어의 정의(定義), 연어법(連語法) 및 예문(例文)을 소개하는 귀납적 문제 해결 방법으로 꾸며놓았다.

● 각 장의 「숙어의 해설(Explanation of the Idioms)」항에는 숙어의 정의(Definition)」와 연어법(Collocation) 그리고 예문(Sample Sentences)이 수록되어 있는데, 이 한국어 주석·증보판에서는 이것들을 대폭 증보한 후 그 번역과 주석을 붙여 놓아 영어 실력이 약한 중급 수준 이하의 학습자에게도 도움이 되도록 배려하였다.

● 제17장 부록에는 숙어의 이해에 필요한 문법용어의 설명과 16종의 숙어 구문형을 도해와 예문을 통해 일목요연하게 설명하는 동시에 그 용법에 대한 유의 사항도 덧붙여 놓았는데, 이 장은 전문이 한국어로 번역되어 있다.

● 각장의 연습문제에 대한 해답을 제시하고, 이 책에서 다룬 숙어들의 적절한 예문들을 각종 문헌과 사전들에서 골라 한국어 번역문과 주석을 붙여 별책으로 꾸며놓았다.

|연락처| 한국내 판권보유 : **(주) 외국어연수사**

서울特別市 永登浦區 汝矣島洞35-2 (白象빌딩1006號) ☎ 785-0919. 785-1749

서강대학교 영어교육연구소 연구협찬/(주) 외국어연수사 간

Common Problems in KOREAN ENGLISH
한국식 영어의 허점과 오류

이 책의 목적은 한국식 영어의 허점과 오류를 바로 잡아주고 「자연스럽고 (natural), 적응성이 풍부하며(flexible), 관용적인(idiomatic)」영어 표현을 익히도록 하려는 것이다. 그러므로 이 책은 영어를 자주 써야하는 분들이나 각급학교 영어선생님들과 올바른 영어 표현을 익히고자 하는 학생들에게 유익한 참고서나 길잡이가 될 것이다.

특   색

- 한국식 영어 특유의 오용 사례를 정선한 후 그 원인을 밝혀내어 상세히 설명하고 올바른 표현법을 구체적으로 예시하였다.
- 오용 사례를 (1) 문법적 오류 (2) 낱말 뜻의 혼동 (3) 어색하거나 부적절한 표현의 3편으로 나누어 그 잘못을 지적하고 올바른 문장으로 고쳐 놓았으며, 그 대안으로 다양한 표현방법을 풍부한 예문으로 제시했을 뿐 아니라 방대한 연습문제를 만들고 그 모범답안까지 제시해 두었다.
- 내용설명은 물론 예문과 대화례(sample sentences and dialogs) 등이 저자 특유의 간명한 필치로 씌어져 있어 이해하기 쉽고 활용도 용이하다.
- 각 문제점의 요점을 간추려 우리말로 옮겨 놓았으며 교실 수업과 자습 양용에 적합하도록 만들었다.

저   자

David Kosofsky는 The University of Maryland에서 서양사를 전공했고(B.A.) Brandeis University에서 비교 역사학을 전공했으며(M.A.) 미국, 일본 및 말레이지아에서 영어를 가르쳤고 1982년에 내한한 이래 서강대학교 영어교육연구소에서 Advanced Seminar class를 가르치면서 영어학습교재의 연구개발에 전념하고 있다. 그는 The Asian Wall Street Journal과 Asiaweek에 기고하면서 소설도 써 왔다.

단시일내에 미국 본토인의 빠른 대화
청취에 적응할 수 있는 최신
청취력 개발 코오스

Listen for It
Task-based American English Listening Course

영자 신문은 읽을수 있는데, AFKN 방송은 이해가 안가는 분, TOFEL이나 TOEIC의 Listening Comprehension 성적이 향상되지 않는 분, 미국인 교수의 강의를 거의 알아 듣지 못하는 분은 처음부터 이 교재로 빠른 대화 듣기 적응훈련을 받으면 단시일내에 고민이 해결될 것입니다.

고교 상급반이나 대학생들은 선배들의 전철을 밟지 말고 지금부터 이 교재로 청취 훈련을 받으면 선배들처럼 시간을 낭비하지 않고 빠른 시일내에 미국인과의 대화는 물론 미국인 교수의 강의를 들을 수 있는 확고한 기초가 생길 것입니다.

이 교재는 일상적 관심사를 화제(topic)로 삼아 미국인들이 다양한 기능(function)으로 이야기하는 대화에 토대를 두고 있기 때문에 그대로 일상회화에 응용할 수 있읍니다.

이 교재는 고등학교 상급반이나 대학 또는 성인영어회화 과정에 적합하도록 다음과 같이 4부로 꾸며져 있읍니다.

Starting out : 화재를 소개하고 대화의 배경을 이루는 정보를 제공하며 대화를 이해 하는데 필요한 표현(낱말・숙어 등)을 설명.

Listening for : 화제(topic)와 관련된 몇 가지의 과제 해결에 토대를 둔 청취 활동.

Trying it out : 실제로 회화에 응용해서 말해보는 활동.

이 교재를 자력으로 공부하고자 하는 분들은 녹음대본과 설문의 해답이 수록된 별책 자습서를 이용하면 좋을 것입니다.

총판 : (株)外國語研修社
서울시 영등포구 여의도동 35-2
백상빌딩 1006호
Tel : 785-0919, 785-1749

교재의 구성 : Student Book : 1권 자습서 : 1권 Tape : C-60 8개

미국 영어회화의 최고봉을 정복하는
OXFORD AMERICAN ENGLISH COURSE

JACK C. RICHARDS DAVID BYCINA

PERSON TO PERSON
Communicative Speaking and Listening Skills

© Oxford University Press, Book 1, 1984; Book 2, 1985

교재 구성 : Book1 : Student Book 1권, 자습서 1권, 테잎 6개
Book2 : Student Book 1권, 자습서 1권, 테잎 6개

1 OXFORD가 특별히 한국과 일본 영어학도들의 취약점을 연구한 끝에 Communicative Speaking & Listening Skills 연마에 역점을 두고 개발한 Best Seller로 大學生/ 一般成人用의 영어회화 최종완성 Course.

2 각 Unit마다 1. Presentation Dialogue〔대화〕2. Give It A Try〔연습〕3. Listen to This〔청취〕로 나누어, 전 30 Units에 걸쳐 110종의 다양한 Topics를 148 종의 Communicative Function으로 엮은 Functional Course의 결정판.

3 Stress(강세), Intonation(음조) 및 Rhythm(음률) 등 초분절음소의 철저한 학습과 Communicative Skills 습득에 필수적인 특수 구문 및 어법의 집중 훈련에 주안점을 둔 새로운 교재.

4 실용/학술의 각국면을 생생하게 연출하여 12개의 Cassette에 압축한 입체음향 교재로 Communicative Speaking은 물론, Tasks, Note—taking, Gap—filling, Dialogue Completion 및 Multiple Choice 등의 연습을 통하여 구미 유학에 지장이 없는 청취력을 양성하는 Course로 TOEFL, 취직시험 등 각종 영어시험 대비용으로도 최적.

연락처 한국내 총판 : (주) 외국어연수사

서울特別市 永登浦區 汝矣島洞35-2(白象빌딩1006號) ☎ 785-0919. 785-1749

최신간 AMERICAN ENGLISH Course

EAST WEST (1~3권)
© Oxford University Press 1989

3단계 과정(3권)으로 구성된 EAST-WEST는 중—상급 수준의 성인용 영어회화 과정으로서 **의사 소통 기능의 향상**을 주목적으로 개발된 것이다. **문법, 기능, 주제, 상황** 등을 골고루 **통합**한 이상적 교수요목(syllabus)에 토대를 두고 있어, 이 교재는, 의사 소통 능력 향상을 위하여 용의 주도하게 통제된 학습 활동을 통하여, **말하고 듣는 연습**을 철저히 할 수 있도록 꾸며져 있다.

특 장

1 모든 영어 회화 교육에 적합하나 특히 말하기를 꺼리는 학생들에게나 학생수가 많은 경우에 크게 도움이 된다.
2 전 교과를 통해서 자연스런 언어를 사용했으나, 이와 다르거나 대안으로 쓰일 표현도 유의 했다.
3 미국 생활의 여러 국면을 소개하기 위해 culture capsules 란을 두었다.
4 학생들의 관심을 끌고, 생활 체험을 이용하며, 솔선하여 말을 하도록 유도하는 의사 소통 중심의 교재이다.
5 언어의 내용을 반복하면서 회화력을 육성하는 과정과 과제를 푸는 과정에서 학생들에게 필요한 여러가지 도움을 주고 있다.
6 두 사람이나 소집단의 역할놀이와 빈칸에 적합한 말을 넣는 연습문제들이 광범하게 사용되었다.

단원의 구성

● 총 14단원으로 구성되어 있는 총천연색의 학생용 교재는 각 단원의 8쪽씩으로 되어 있다.
● 각 단원은 각 단원의 교수 요점을 소개하는 대화로 시작된다.
● 다음 4쪽에는 발음 연습을 포함하여 정확성과 유창성의 향상을 노리는 말하는 연습이 따른다.
● 다음에는 문법상의 요점, 상황에 맞는 표현, 기능[목적] 및 개념에 적합한 표현과 각 단원에 쓰인 숙어적 표현등을 요약하는 Checklist 란이 있다.
● 마지막 두쪽은 수동적 기능인 청취력과 독해력을 향상시키기 위한 것이다.
● 제1권에는 Moon of India라는 추리 소설을 14편으로 나누어 각 단원마다 실어 독자의 흥미를 유발하고 독서의 즐거움을 맛보게 해 준다.
● East West 는 각 권마다 학생용의 교재 및 연습장, 교사용 교재와 카셋트로 되어 있다. 별도로 Moon of India 의 카셋트도 있다.

판매대행 : **(주) 외국어연수사**
서울 영등포구 여의도동 35-2 백상빌딩 1006호
☎ 785-0919, 1749, 780-2817

최신간 AMERICAN ENGLISH Course

ON COURSE(1~2권)

© Oxford University Press 1989

■ 2단계로 되어 있는 **On Course**는 초급-중급 수준의 **성인용** 영어 회화 과정으로서 **말하고 듣는** 기능을 중심으로 꾸며진 편리한 교재이다.

■ 학생용 교재는 **30단원**으로 구성되어 있는데 각 단원은 2쪽씩이다. 그래서 사용하기가 아주 편리하며 **50분간**에 학습을 마칠 수 있도록 꾸며져 있다.

■ 또한 학생 상호간의 연습 기회를 제공하기 위하여 두 사람이 **역할 놀이**를 하는 것과 빈칸에 알맞는 말을 넣어 대화를 완성하는 **연습 문제**가 마련되어 있다.

■ 그리고 5단원씩 묶어서 요약하여 연습하는 총 24쪽의 6개 **요약단원 (Summary Units)**이 있는데, 이것들은 30단원에 걸쳐 제시된 재료와 자연스럽게 재 결합하여 이를 보강해 준다.

■ 각 요약 단원마다 **청취력 향상**을 위한 **과제 중심의 연습** 문제가 수록되어 있다.

판매대행 : **(주)외국어연수사**

서울 영등포구 여의도동 35-2
백상빌딩 1006호
☎ 785-0919, 1749, 780-2817

SMALL TALK
OXFORD UNIVERSITY PRESS 1986.CAROLYN GRAHAM저
Cassette 2개, 교재1권으로 미국영어 특유의 발음을 Jazz Chant로 배우는 최신간

그릇된 발음으로 영어를 배운 기간이 길면 길수록 그것이 영어 청취력과 회화력 향상에 큰 장애가 된다는 것은 ESL/EFL 교사들 모두가 통감하고 있는 사실이다. 이 문제를 근본적으로 해결하려는 시도에서 마련된 것이 이 교재이다.

이 교재는 미국영어의 정확한 발음, 특히 강세(Stress), 음조(Intonation), 음률(Rhythm)과 연음(Blending)및 축약음(Contraction)의 학습에 중점을 두고 있다.

특히 본문의 대화(Dialog)를 Jazz 노래가락으로 만들어 녹음해 놓았기 때문에 노래를 배우듯이 이것을 따라 부르다 보면 자신도 모르게 Native Speaker와 같은 회화력을 습득할 수 있다.

이 교재는 주로 한국어·일본어 등과 같은 **음절어(Syllabic Language)**를 쓰는 국민들이 **음률어(Rhythmic Language)**인 영어의 정확한 발음 특히 음조, 강세, 음률등을 습득하는데 경이적인 효과를 나타내고 있어 전세계 영어 교육계의 주목을 끌고 있다.

Cassette 1

세계적으로 유명한 Jazz 음악가들이 연주한 Jazz 음악을 배경으로 교재 본문이 노래가락으로 녹음되어 있다.

Cassette 2

Cassette 1의 본문을 응용한 다양한 청취 연습과 Word Puzzle로 된 흥미 진진한 청취 연습 문제가 수록되어 있다.

저자 Carolyn Graham은 New York University의 교수로서 The American Language Institute에서 ESL(English as a second language)을 가르치고 있으며 Jazz를 활용한 Jazz Chants(1978), Jazz Chants for Children(1979), 및 The Electric Elephant(1982)등의 영어회화 교재를 저술한바 있다.

한국내총판 : (주)외국어연수사